The Forest of Bowland

Little Bowland, Lower Hodder Valley and Trough of Bowland

by

JOHN DIXON

'The Roving Recusant'

With illustrations by
JANNA JÄRVINEN & JOHN DIXON

The Forest of Bowland
Little Bowland, Lower Hodder Valley & Trough of Bowland

By John Dixon

With illustrations by
Janna Järvinen & John Dixon

Copyright © John Dixon 2004
All rights reserved

Published by Aussteiger Publications

Typeset by Sophie Dixon
And copy read by Barbara Carne

Printed by
Lamberts Print & Design, Station Road, Settle,
North Yorkshire BD24 9AA

First Edition 2004

ISBN 1 872764 10 X

For Wayne and Maxine

Distributors: Lancashire Books, 213 Chorley Old Road,
Whittle-le-Woods, Chorley PR6 7NP. Tel. 01247-278613

Internet: www.lancsbooks.co.uk
The Historic Lancashire Organisation
'Promoting the Real Lancashire'

PLEASE OBSERVE THE COUNTRY CODE

AUSSTEIGER PUBLICATIONS

Contents

INTRODUCTION 4

WALK 1   **LITTLE SWITZERLAND**
              Dunsop Bridge, Hareden, Mellor Knoll & Whitewell
              8 miles, allow 5 hours with lunch 6

WALK 2   **OUR LADY OF THE FELLS....**
              Dunsop Bridge, Whitewell, Crimpton & Knowlmere
              7½ miles, allow 5 hours with lunch 16

WALK 3 & 4 **ABOVE THE WHITEWELL GORGE**
       3)   Whitewell, Fair Oak, Chipping & Dinkling Green
              7 miles, allow 5 hours with lunch 26
       4)   Whitewell, Stakes, Greystoneley & Fair Oak
              6 miles, 4 hours 40

WALK 5 & 6 **ONCE DEER DID ROAM & ROMANS MARCH**
       5)   Whitewell, Stakes, The Lees & Radholme
              5 miles, 3 hours 48
       6)   Whitewell, Stakes, The Lees & Browsholme
              9 miles, 6 hours 55

WALK 7   **AROUND THE FEATHER BED**
              Dunsop Bridge, Sykes, Brennand & Whitendale
              7 or 9 miles, 5 to 6 hours 61

WALK 8   **HEART OF BOWLAND**
              Langden Castle, Fair Snape, Parlick & Dinkling Green
              16 miles, 8 hours 70

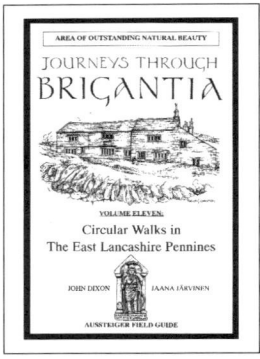 

John Dixon is available for leading day, and weekend walks, throughout the year. John also lectures on the Bowland-Pennine region through organised field trips.

Contact Aussteiger for details & availability.

Information: www.lancsbooks.co.uk

Tel: 01200 443129   Aussteiger Publications

The Writers Bookshop: www.mulberrybooks.com

Right to Roam: openaccess@countryside.gov.uk

LANCASHIRE HISTORY QUARTERLY
www.hudson-history.co.uk

INTRODUCTION

> "The trouble today is that not enough people are leaning over five-barred gates. Whenever I lean over a five-barred gate, I always ruminate. And whenever I ruminate the world seems a better place."
>
> *George Birthill, 1967*

George's sentiment was a familiar one with my Grandad Dixon's generation. Grandad walked to work every day from our family home at Mill Hill in Livesey to Preston and back in the evening, and thought nothing of it. On a Sunday he would walk up to Tockholes talking to everyone he met along the way, and I would follow him. "If you can't keep up, I'm not waiting for you." And he meant it. With Grandad I learned how to walk and how to converse with all and sundry.

> "In my father's house, we breakfasted on maize porridge; at mid-day we ate potatoes; in the evening bacon soup, and that every day of the week. And despite the economists who praised the English diet, we, with that vegetarian feeding, were fat and strong. Do you know why? Because we breathed the air of our fields and lived from the produce of out own cultivation."
>
> *Pierre-Joseph Proudhon, 1864*

As far as possible, I eat food that is grown or reared in Lancashire, readily available in season at local markets. To maintain a good head of hair I eat kelp from the Norwegian Sea. I avoid wheat products as they lead to ill-health for Northern Europeans, rye and oat bread promote good health and well-being. 'Early to bed, early to rise', is the maxim to follow. Television dulls the mind, corrupts and controls behaviour and is to be avoided at all cost. Walking is by far the finest form of exercise that the human being can take and it costs very little. Leave the car at home and use local transport – the Forest of Bowland is very well served in this regard. Well, that's all for now. Enjoy your walking.

John Dixon, Clitheroe 2004

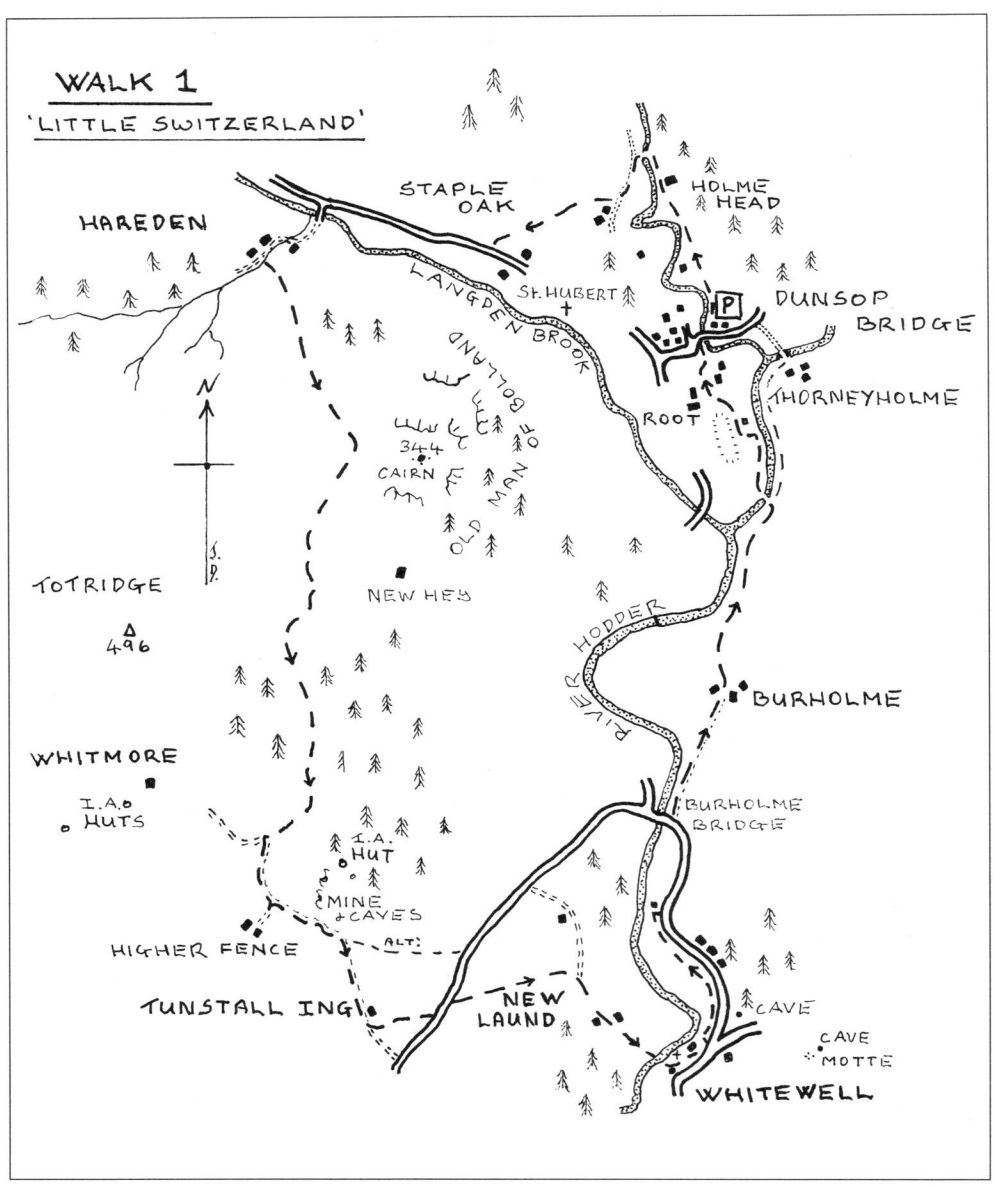

WALK 1
LITTLE SWITZERLAND

8 miles easy walking, the only climb being from Hareden to the Totridge-Mellor Knoll saddle – the rest is pure joy. Allow 5 hours to include a stop at the Inn at Whitewell.

On this walk we climb behind the 'Old Man of Bolland' to gain superb views that have led to this part of the Hodder Valley being described as a 'Little Switzerland'. Later we descend to Whitewell crossing the Hodder by the way of 'hipping-stones'. Our return is up-river visiting the Deserted Mediaeval Village site of Burholme, then back for a brew at Puddleducks.

Walk along the lane by the side of the Post Office, passing the children's activity area to the rear of Holme Head cottages.

The winner of the 1861 Derby, Kettledrum, was stabled here at Holme Head and was trained in the fields at Root Farm.

Pass through the gate and walk on to go over a footbridge.

Look out for the dipper bobbing from stone to stone. It has a white bib and chocolate-brown plumage.

Turn left and walk along the road almost to the cattle-grid at Closes farm. Walk into the field on your right and walk around the pens to pass through an old Towneley estate gate.

This is a pheasant breeding area, the poults are hand reared. The birds are reared for sport and are a feature of the local economy. The pheasant is a descendant of an ancient Asian jungle fowl. The mating call is a loud, metallic 'korrk-kok'.

Walk on by the wall side to the corner above Staple Oak barn.

The Hareden Valley now comes into view. The hillside over to the left was once a rabbit warren, the skins for use in the local hat-making industry.

Walk on and over to the right to go through gate at the bridleway sign onto the Trough road.

The roadway beyond the cattle-grid is the start of that wild mountain pass known as the Trough of Bowland, the side valleys being once refuge of Jacobite outlaws.

Abbot Paslew of Whalley Abbey (for his part in the ill fated Pilgrimage of Grace) was brought in chains this way to be tried for Treason at Lancaster Castle. His body was brought back along the Trough road to be displayed at Little Imps field at Whalley.

Right, and walk up the road to cross the river bridge at Hareden. Follow the farm lane to cross a stone bridge and walk on to the kennels where the dogs bark in unison as we pass.

HAREDEN

It is always a joy to walk up the chestnut lined avenue into the tiny hamlet of Hareden – the surrounding fells draw one in to their hidden recesses and high redoubts that once provided shelter to fugitives of old.

HAREDEN

The hamlet started life as a grange of Kirkstall Abbey for the breeding of draught oxen in the early 1300's. The buildings we see today date to the 17th century when the Harrison and Knowle families farmed here. The main house is dated W.H. 1690.

Cross the river bridge and pass over stile by gate. Walk up to the left to go over stile by gate in left-hand wall. Walk up the

track 20 paces to head up to the right to finally pick up a green track that leads on up to pass over a stile by gate below the rise of Mellor Knoll.

Mellor Knoll – the 'bare hill', is said to be the site of a Roman signal station from which Totridge Fell, 'the look-out hill', takes its name. On the flanks of the knoll are many ancient bell-pits where lead was once sought. The summit of the knoll is topped by a small cairn and offers fine views over the Hodder Valley.

Walk up the track then fork right and along the saddle to go over a ladder-stile near a gate in the far wall.

Superb walking and great views from now on, so savour to the full.

The path leads on and down to enter wood via gate. The path takes us above Hodder Valley to enter Whitemore plantation via gate.

Our path leads us through the quiet pinewood to leave by a field-gate. Walk on to meet the Whitemore farm lane at the hen huts.

These free-range, corn fed hens lay the finest eggs in Bowland – a real treat.

Above us is the lovely fellside farmstead of Whitemore. Is a finer setting possible?

Standing forlorn by a field wall at Whitemore is an iron-shod old peat/turf sledge. These were used to bring the peat turfs down from the felltop haggs to be dried out for fuel.

To the south-west of the farmstead is the site of an Iron Age homestead. Another is located above the caves at Whitemore Knot.

Left, and walk along the lane to go left at the junction...

The hidden village of Dinkling Green lies over to the right.

...and walk on to pass further hen huts to just beyond the limestone reef of Long Knots.

A path leaves the lane here and goes down to pass through a gate, and on directly down to pass through another gate onto the road leading to Burholme Bridge. Those who do not wish to cross the hipping stones at Whitewell may wish to use this path.

A green track to the left leads to the old calamine mines and limestone quarries. These caves are frought with danger, and along with nearby Whitemore Pot should not be entered or approached.

Continue along the lane to Tunstall Ing.

The view looking up the Hodder Valley from the farmstead here is magnificent and I am pleased to have finally included it on a regular trail.

The place named 'Tunstall' refers to a very ancient farm that once stood nearby – a Romano-British settlement sheltered by the limestone knots. The 'Ing' refers to the hill behind.

After crossing the cattle-grid, walk into the field on the left to pass the fence corner towards the hillside quarry opposite, and carry on over a fence-stile onto the road. Left, and pass through field-gate on the right. Walk over to the left, around the hillside to pass through steel field-gate. Follow right-hand fence down though field-gate and down the track to the farm lane and old cheese-press via gate.

NEW LAUND FARM

Since the historian Margaret Panakar began to highlight the old craft of rural cheese making and the methods and equipment used, old cheese presses have begun to sprout up as objects of rustic art in the Lancashire and Bowland landscapes. Lancashire cheese is the finest produced in the British Isles, and over three hundred varieties can be found. A visit to the Lancashire Cheese Museum at Chipping will prove most enlightening.

NEW LAUND FARM

The farm started life as a keeper's cottage in the days of the great forest, and the inhabitants used the hipping-stones in the bed of the River Hodder to reach the manor and court house at Whitewell. Until recently the stones were long gone, but public pressure had forced a reluctant Lancashire County Council to replace them as part of our footpath heritage.

Pass through the farmyard at New Laund to leave by the field-gate. Walk down to the right to cross the hipping-stones.

This area, known as the Whitewell Gorge, is home ground to roe deer. The roe is a relative new comer, sika being most common in the area, having moved over Bowland from the Lune Valley. The buck has small antlers reflecting its small size. The caudal disc, in contrast to that of the sika, is kidney-shaped and mostly white. A gruff bark is the alarm call of the roe buck.

Badgers have their setts in the quiet woodland of the gorge. Here, undisturbed by man, they emerge in the last hours of daylight in search of fresh bracken to replace old bedding. In Spring a sow badger will have her cubs with her on these forays.

Pass over stile by gate and walk to the left to pass through the water garden via gate.

The White Well is over on the right.

Walk up to the Inn at Whitewell.

THE INN AT WHITEWELL

THE INN AT WHITEWELL

The Whitewell Hotel is one of the very few inns that can be described as a true country hostelry. The layout is friendly and informal; gentry, yeoman and fieldworker sup shoulder to shoulder, and the repast served is of a very high standard and most reasonably priced. I always opt for the succulent Bolland Pie with new potatoes and greens followed by a few measures of the local waters.

The oldest part of the inn was once the manor at Whitewell; the Swainmote and Woodmote Courts met there. Then the Master Forester or his deputy the Bow Bearer, presided with a jury made up of Forest keepers to hear claims and disputes that had been brought to their notice. Around the courthouse there would be much seasonal activity such as markets and fairs. The inn is still the meeting place of most local social gatherings, even for church meetings.

Walk to the end of the inn to pick up a concessionary path by the Dunsop road. The path takes us above the river passing the remains of a former bridge.

Here a spring bridge once spanned the Hodder. It was 100ft. long and stood some 12ft. above the Hodder. In July 1906, when about fifty well-heeled and well-sloshed trippers were on it, the bridge gave way in two places plunging then into the sobering waters below, luckily without loss of life.

Walk on and pass over a footbridge and enter the field via a kissing-gate. Follow the right-hand boundary on some way to pass over a fence-stile onto the road. Walk up the road to

Burholme Bridge.

We are now standing in the former West Riding of Yorkshire. Across the bridge is old historic Lancashire. An old West Riding iron boundary marker can be found on the other side of the river claiming the bridge for Yorkshire.

Walk along the farm track to Burholme farm.

BURHOLME

Though today only a single farmstead, Burholme was once a thriving village with its own church and manor house.

The Norman Survey of 1086 records a settlement hereabouts called 'Bogewrde' – the first element being 'bow' (bend in a river as in Bowland), the second being 'Wearda', Old Norse 'voroa', meaning beacon or cairn.

The site of the cairn or beacon could have been Kitcham Hill or Mellor Knoll, possibly a former Roman signal station given its close proximity to the Roman Road between Ribchester and Overbrough.

The Norman Survey records Bowland as a small discrete estate with its caput at Grindleton, with 16 dependant berewicks as a sub-section of Craven. Before the Danish/Norse wars it was part of a vast estate known as Blackburnshire (c.923), only after was it included in the diocese of York (Northumbria).

The origins of the Domesday settlements of Bowland go back to a time when Blackburnshire was a vast estate, part of a greater unit – the Celtic-British Kingdom of Rheged (c.590) that ran from the Solway to the Welsh border. The origins of the discrete estate form of land organisation probably lies in the ancient Kingdom of Brigantia. For Brigantia, like Rheged, was a confederation of smaller kingdoms based on discrete estates.

I am of the opinion that Burholme is a strong candidate for the 'lost' Domesday village of Bogewrde, though others suggest Knowlemere and

Birkett. In my lectures and field trips I put the evidence forward for this view.

A font found at Burholme, now in use as a Holy Water stoop at St. Huberts, Dunsop Bridge, points to a church existing here by the 14th century when the monks of Kirkstall Abbey held land here as vaccary (cow pasture). When the Radholme deer park was established the church and court was moved to Whitewell.

With the decline of the deer park, Burholme thrived as a small hamlet, with some six families living here in 1527. By the 17th century Burholme was a centre of non-conformity.

Burholme Font

In 1682 Nicholas Walne, a Quaker, took his wife and family from his parents' farm at Burholme to sail with William Penn on the Welcome for a new life in American where Penn founded Philadelphia and went on to establish the Quaker colony of Pennsylvania in 1683.

Those early Bowland emigrants to the New World named their new settlement after their old village. Burholme is today a suburban district of the city of Philadelphia.

Nicholas, being a member of the first Assembly at Philadelphia, went on to become a member of the first Grand Jury, Sheriff, and Justice of the Courts of Bucks County Pennsylvania.

The Robert Waln Ryerss Library at Burholme Park, Fox Chase, Philadelphia, was built in 1859 by Joseph Waln Ryerss, a descendant of Nicholas, as a residence and left by his son Robert to the City of Philadelphia to be used a as park, library and museum "Free to the people forever".

The barn at Burholme has many inscribed stones that bear much faded dates and inscriptions and are refered to as 'Quaker Stones'. One, below the

initials of Thomas Swinhulhurst 1619, is inscribed:
I JANE LOVE FOR TRU TO W*** AND
FAITHFUL I WILL BE (Jane Walne, wife of
Nicholas Walne).

Beyond the farmhouse turn left to pass over footbridge and through field gate. Walk along the brow to pass over stile by gate. Continue on to pass over two more stiles by gates, then follow the path on to cross the green iron bridge.

The bridge is a good place to spot the oystercatcher, a black and white wader with bright orange-red legs and bill.

Burholme

Above us to the west stands Mellor Knoll, know locally as 'The Old Man of Bolland'. Viewed from here the hill has the appearance of a rotund gentleman sleeping the afternoon away after a dinner-time session in the Whitwell. During the summer months the leafy foliage on the north end give the Old man a fine crop of curly hair.

Follow the river up to go left at wall and over fence-stile. Walk round the corner and follow the track...

The small building on your right is a stable with two corner wooden mangers. The field here is where Kettledrum, winner of the 1861 Derby, was exercised by the Towneley family of Burnley.

...to go over stile at gateway. Walk up the banking to go over ladder-stile. Walk on to go over next ladder-stile.

Below us stands Root Farm. The upper floor of the buttressed barn was at one time the local dance hall known as the 'Root Ball Room'.

Walk down and follow the lane to Dunsop Bridge.

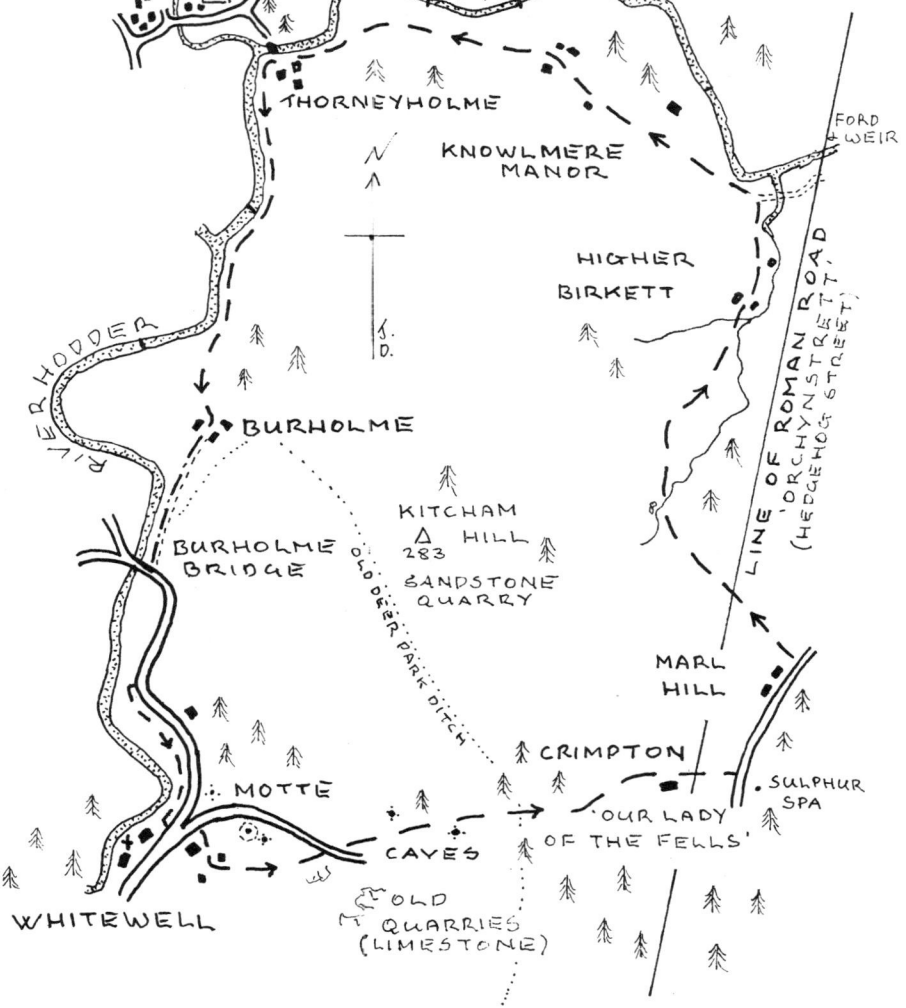

Little Bowland, Lower Hodder Valley & Trough of Bowland

WALK 2
'OUR LADY OF THE FELLS'

- DUNSOP BRIDGE
- RIVER HODDER
- THORNEYHOLME
- KNOWLMERE MANOR
- HIGHER BIRKETT
- FORD & WEIR
- BURHOLME
- KITCHAM HILL △ 283
- SANDSTONE QUARRY
- BURHOLME BRIDGE
- OLD DEER PARK DITCH
- LINE OF ROMAN ROAD ('ORCHYNSTRETT') (HEDGEHOG STREET)
- MARL HILL
- CRIMPTON
- SULPHUR SPA
- MOTTE
- CAVES
- 'OUR LADY OF THE FELLS'
- OLD QUARRIES (LIMESTONE)
- WHITEWELL

Little Bowland, Lower Hodder Valley & Trough of Bowland

WALK 2
OUR LADY OF THE FELLS

7½ miles easy walking with one gentle climb between Whitewell and Crimpton Plantation. Allow 5 hours to enjoy a small repast at the Inn at Whitewell.

After a riverside stroll down the Hodder we will take in the charms of Whitewell followed by a romp up the hillside to the lovely farmstead of Crimpton – 'Our Lady of the Fells'. Our decent to Dunsop is by way of Birkett and Knowlmere, both holding a fascination of their own. All in all, a rewarding day out.

DUNSOP TO WHITEWELL

On leaving the car park turn left and walk along the road a short way, to go right, along the avenue of Wellingtonia and cross the bridge at Thorneyholme. Pass through the gate on the right and follow the river down, over two fence-stiles to the green, iron footbridge. Follow the path over the rough ground...

Here the Hodder is met by the Langden Brook while the Old Man of Bolland sleeps on with Totridge keeping a 'look out' over the Hodder Valley. Notice the old hipping stones that cross the river to Langden Holme.

...to go over stile by old Water Authority iron gate. Cross the field to pass over stile by gate and on to go over further stile by gate. Walk up to enter Burholme farmyard via stile and footbridge.

BURHOLME

The farmhouse today at Burholme incorporates two early 17th century cottages and was remodelled in the early 19th century. Notice the huge gable

chimney stack.

Archaeological excavations to find the 'lost village' and chapel at Burholme were undertaken in 1985/86. The site of the chapel was located along with eight former buildings and a circular structure thought to be a pinfold.

The higher barn at Burholme is also of great interest. The timbers of the cow stalls come from old dismantled ships brought down from Glasson Dock in the 18th century.

Behind this barn the old village well stands in a small enclosure. Though now dry, it was once fed from a natural spring.

Burholme is a working farm. So we shall show respect and not go wandering all over the show in search of all that is to be found here.

Pass through the farmyard and follow the farm lane to Burholme Bridge. Walk down the road to pass over the hedge-stile on the right. A concessionary path follows the left-hand boundary to the Inn at Whitewell via Kissing-gate and footbridge.

THE CHURCH OF ST MICHAEL THE ARCHANGEL

A chapel, dedicated to the Blessed Virgin Mary, was established at the 'White Well of the Cistercian order (Whalley Abbey)' in c.1400 by Walter de Urswyck, Keeper of the Royal Forest of Bowland.

St. MICHAEL, WHITEWELL

Urswyck was Constable of Richmond and Keeper of the 'New Forest' – a wide tract of virgin ground, moor and scroggland reaching from the north bank of the Swale to Stainmoor and the Tees, and westward across Arkengarthdale to the Pennines.

John of Gaunt, Duke of Lancaster, and Earl of Richmond, granted Walter an annuity of forty pounds a year out of the manors of Catterick and Forest, for his valiant services at the Battle of Navarre in support of the noblesse of Knighthood. His effigy rests on an alter-tomb in Catterick Church.

After the Reformation the chapel was re-dedicated to St. Michael the Archangel and received the revenue formerly given to a chapel of that name which once stood in the grounds of Clitheroe Castle.

Devotion to Our Lady was outlawed by the heretical English Church at this time and the statuette of Our Lady of the White Well was removed by good hands for safety.

The chapel became known as Bolland Chapel and was rebuilt and enlarged as we see it today in 1817. The small window in the boiler house on the north side, displaying Perpendicular tracery, is all that remains of the former Roman Catholic chapel.

Inside the chapel a good example of a Jacobean style pulpit can be viewed along with a large tapestry that depicts Christ's descent from the Cross, based on painting by Rubins which is on view in Antwerp Cathedral.

Until April 1974 the parish was partly in the County Palatine of Lancaster and partly in the West Riding of Yorkshire, the River Hodder being the border between the two shires. Notice the Red Rose and the White Rose in the window of the south aisle.

Before you leave the church read the words of Joan Pomfret framed on the north aisle wall, then look around the outside of the church to find where the swallows nest.

A ROMAN OR BRONZE AGE CAMP AT WHITEWELL?

W. Thompson Watkin in his book 'Roman Lancashire' 1883, states that "according the Lewis's 'Topographical Dictionary (7th Ed. 1849)', remains of a Roman camp existed at Whitewell." Whitaker in his 'History of Whalley' records that "opposite Whitewell Keeper's House, remains of a small encampment and a cairn of stones containing Kist vaen and a skeleton were found." Could both authors be referring to the same site and what, if anything, exists today?

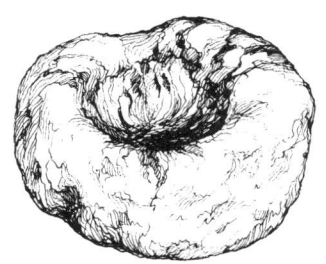
THE WHITEWELL STONE.

In 1984 a large hollowed-out rounded stone was found in the river near to the inn. Upon inspection, archaeologists have declared the stone to be a mortar for the grinding of food grains and date it to the Bronze Age period. Others of learning think that it may once have been a Holy Water font or stoop, worn beyond identification by the waters of Hodder. The object is now known as the 'Whitewell Stone' and can be seen on display in the chapel.

WHITEWELL TO CRIMPTON

Walk up the road by the Village Hall to go up the steps on the right, and through a gate. Walk up to the right of the house and then past the rear of the house to follow the line of trees up to pass through a field-gate.

To the left, above the rise of Hall Hill, Seed Hill Plantation sits atop a knoll of limestone. Lancaster University Archaeological Unit have this site recorded as a 'motte', an earth castle of early date. Local tradition holds that a fortified structure was erected here in the old Radholme Deer Park at the time of James 1. All very intriguing.

In a hollow at the base of the knoll is Whitewell Pot, and as with all the caves we shall pass it should not be entered or approached.

Walk directly on, then to the left to pass through gate onto road by the old limekiln.

These small field kilns were used to produce lime to make mortar for building or to spread on the land to improve the soil.

Pass over stile opposite and walk to the right to go over ladder-stile by trees.

Whitewell Cave is located in a prominent scar amongst the trees. Keep away.

Walk over to the left, and up to the left of the clump of trees.

Within the clump of trees is the open shaft of Hell Hole Pot. Keep well away.

Walk up the hillside to pass over ladder-stile into plantation

Look back to obtain good views of Totridge, Mellor Knoll and the Trough of Bowland.

Pass through the pines to leave by fence-stile on left. Walk over to the right...

Kitcham Hill is in good view. The quarries there provided the red sandstone to build Browsholme Hall.

...over ditch and on to pass through gates above Crimpton. Walk on to enter farmyard via gate (ignore muddy suggested diversion). Walk over to the front of the house.

CRIMPTON FARM, 'OUR LADY OF THE FELLS'

It was to Crimpton that the wooden image of Our Lady of the White Well was brought for safety after the Reformation. The farm was well known to Roman Catholic pilgrims and became refered to as 'Our Lady of the Fells'. Countryfolk, in former times, attributed miraculous healing powers to the image and the waters of the sulphur spa at Crimpton.

Notice the first-floor workshop window of seven lights. Handloom weaving was done here in the 18th century, helping to subsidise the meagre hill-farmers' income. A similar set of windows can be located at Browsholme Heights (Batesons) over the fell.

CRIMPTON TO MARL HILL

Follow the farm lane to the road. Left, and walk up the road to Marl Hill.

MARL HILL

Marl Hill is a pleasing plain-fronted house with a date tablet, A.D.1722. A sun-dial stands in the grounds with the initials N T I and a date, 1690. The house is also known as Birkett Moor Farm.

MARL HILL TO HIGHER BIRKETT

MARL HILL SUNDIAL

Continue past Marl Hill Byre to pass through gateway on the left at footpath post. Walk on to pass over fence-stile by gateway and continue on and down to go over fence-stile onto the moor. Follow the path down to walk on the right bank of the ancient Holloway (sheep fold below on the left) to ford Cripton Brook by the lone alder tree. Follow the path up and over to the right to pass over ladder-stile by gate.

As you stand atop the stile you can see the head and the belly of the old Man of Bolland over on the left.

Walk directly on and down to pick up a track that leads us down to a ford.

Notice the red sandstone in the river bed – Birkett Stone. A line of red sandstone that runs from Cheshire to Carlisle.

Cross the ford and pass through gate. Walk on into Higher Birkett farmyard.

HIGHER BIRKETT

A plaster moulding above a fireplace in the farmhouse bears the initials of Richard and Alice Leigh with a date, 1686. Richard built the first Independent

Chapel at Newton in 1696. When the chapel was rebuilt the original datestone with Richard's initials was re-sited in the porch of the new chapel.

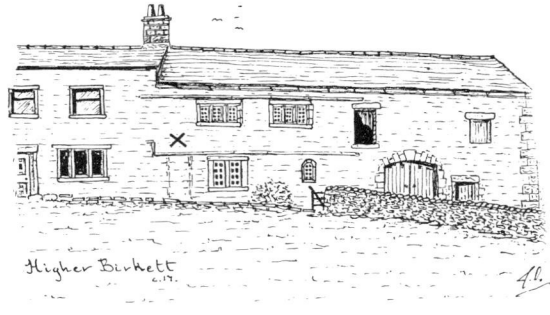

HIGHER BIRKETT TO KNOWLEMERE MANOR

Pass through the gate on the right of the house and through next gate into field. Walk on to the right to pass over ladder-stile. Walk on to the drive by Giddy Bridge. Left, and follow the drive to view Knowlemere Manor.

Sited at Grey Gill, the house is built in the Gothic Style of the Victorian era: with its many gables and chimneys it presents an interesting picture – some refer to it as a 'Calender House', now there is a test for your powers of observation.

The Manor was built by the Peel family, descendants of Sir Robert Peel, founder of the modern Police Force.

KNOWLEMERE TO DUNSOP

Continue along the drive to go over stile by gate at Mossthwaite Farm.

The trackway we are now on is an old coach road that once linked Thorneyholme Hall with the village of Newton.

Follow the track on to go over stile by gate, and on to go over a wall-stile on the right by a gateway. Walk down the field on a left diagonal to go over fence-stile in line of trees. Walk on to pass through gates at riverside and on to the bridge at Thorneyholme.

Built by the Towneley family of Burnley, Thorneyholme was gifted by to the family to the Sisters of Notre Dame, a Roman Catholic teaching order, and became a nunnery – the nuns' Dame School was in the houses by the bridge at Dunsop. The Hall is now an enclave of private dwellings.

Cross the bridge and walk down to Dunsop for a well-earned brew at Puddleducks Post Office Café.

LOWER BIRKETT

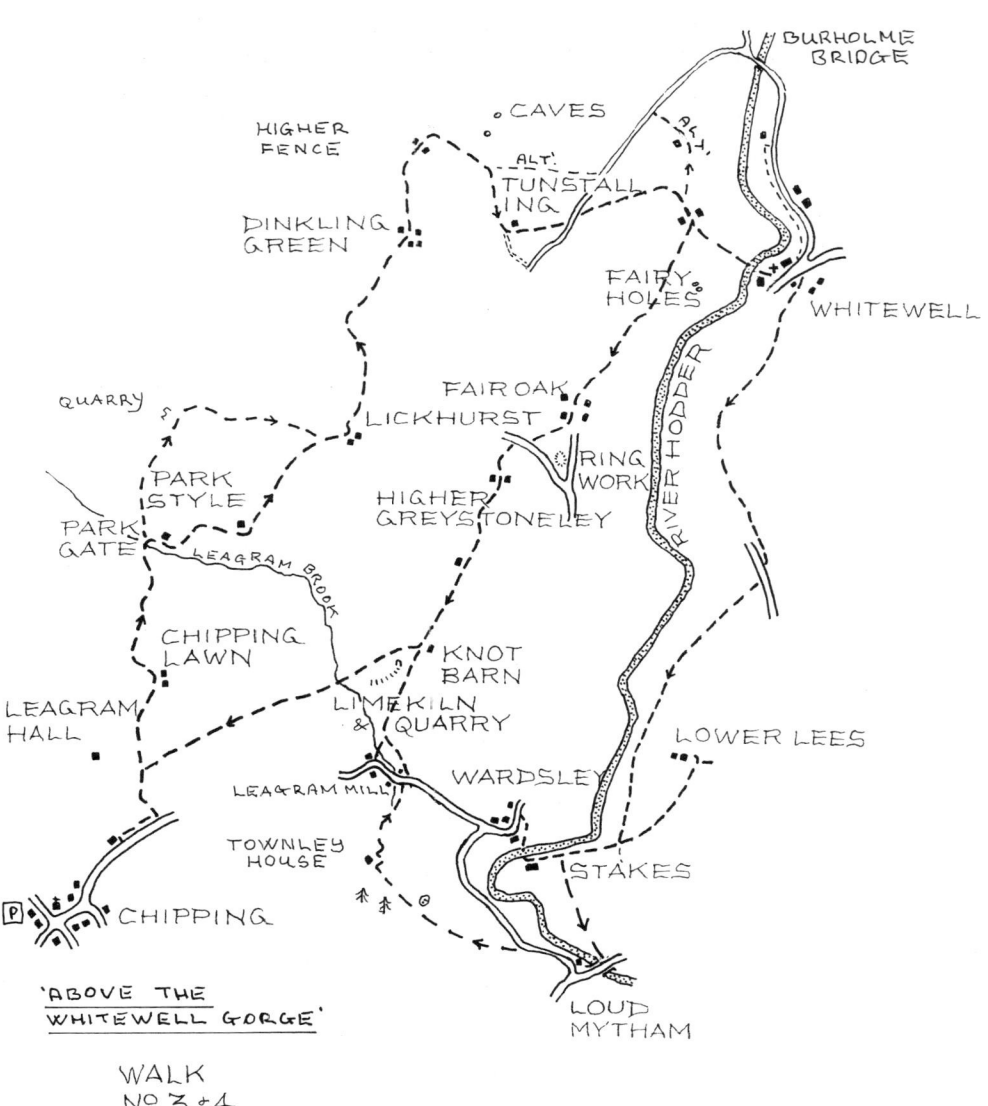

WALK 3 & 4
ABOVE THE WHITEWELL GORGE

Walk 3, 7 miles, can be started at Whitewell or Chipping and takes in Fair Oak and Dinkling Green.

Walk 4, 6 miles, starts at Whitewell, parking down to the left of the church, and takes in Stakes and Fair Oak.

The two can be made into a longer walk of 9 miles by linking at Knot Barn.

The walks involve crossing the Hodder by hipping stones, but alternatives are given if the river is high.

WALK 3
WHITEWELL TO FAIR OAK

This walk takes in the old Leagram Deer Park with a visit to the 'hidden' hamlet of Dinkling Green. With good 'limestone walking' and superb views all the way, this walk, with a stop for a bite to eat at Chipping, makes for a rewarding day out.

Walk down past the church to pass through water-garden via gates. Cross the lawn to pass over stile by gate and cross the hipping-stones. Walk up to enter New Laund via gate. Walk past the house to pass through gate on the left by the wooden shed. We now climb up to the left, up and on to pass over stile by gate.

In the wooded ravine over on your left, sited on the south-east face of an outcrop of limestone, are the three caves known as Fairy Holes.

In 1946, an excavation was carried out on the site by the archaeologist

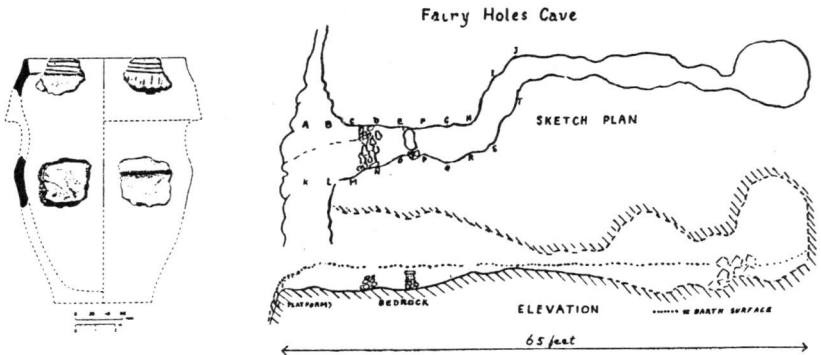

Reginald C. Musson. In front of the larger cave is a flat platform on which evidence of Bronze Age daily life was found. This included animal bones, a pebble pounder (used to extract marrow from bones) and shards of a food vessel/urn.

All that survived of this tripartite collared urn was a large rim-collar shard, two fragments displaying neck/shoulder/body elements and five smaller pieces, probably from the base of the body. This is the only collared urn to have been found in a cave in Lancashire. Its tripartite Pennine form assigns it to an Early Bronze Age Date.

Aerial photography has identified a number of possible settlement sites in the area between Dinkling Green and the Hodder at Whitewell and in the area around Whitmore below Totridge. The largest of these sites is at Fair Oak farm.

Our path leads up and over the rim of New Laund Hill, down to the right to pass over a ladder-stile. Walk around by the fence on the right to enter farm track via field-gate. Follow the track to Fair Oak farm.

FAIR OAK

The first house we see at the old vaccary of Fair Oak, locally called

'Farrick', is the Old Coach House of the former Fair Oak House. Above the first floor mullioned window of the gable end, flanked by a dove cote, is a stone tablet inscribed; JOHN PARKINGSON, DOROTHY HIS WIFE, AND THOMAS HIS SON, 1716. A door lintel on the front bears the date 1664, and nearby stands the weight from an old cheese press.

We pass the farmhouse next, built, for the most part, in the early 18th century. Inside are two rather grand stone fireplaces, one of which has a lintel that is a re-used doorhead with the date 1720.

We walk on now to enter the farmyard on the right to view the 'Gunnary', a robust barn, also known as the 'Battery'. Above the main doorway is a date tablet of 1724 with the initials J.D.P. & W.P.. The names 'Gunnary' and 'Battery' come from a time of the 1745 Jacobite Rising.

Many people in the area supported the righteous Jacobite cause, and regularly mustered at Fair Oak for musket practise under their Captain, Jack Parkingson. Even today musket balls often turn up during ploughing.

Righteous insurrection has always been a feature at Fair Oak: old records tell us of one Christopher Harris, who married Mary, daughter and heir of Robert Singlehurst of Fair Oak. Harris took the King's side during the Civil War, and as a 'recusant and delinquent' had his estate sequestered in 1654.

His son took part in the Jacobite Rising of

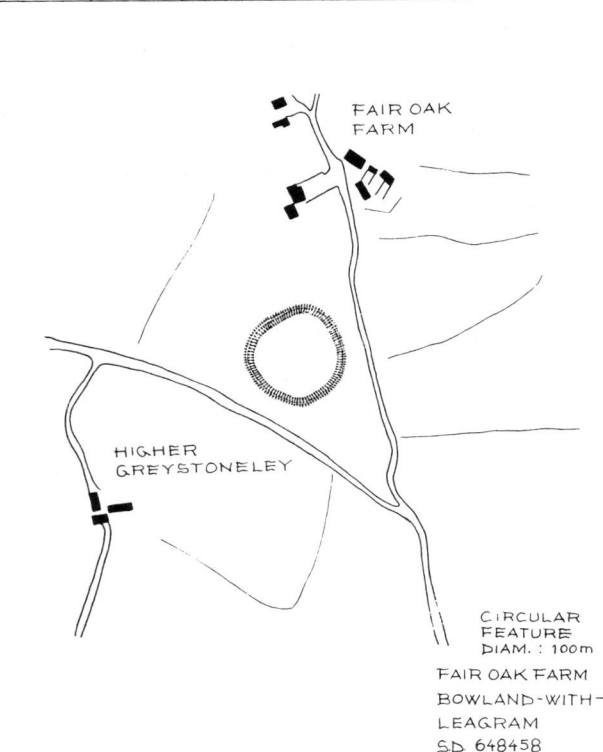

CIRCULAR FEATURE
DIAM. : 100m
FAIR OAK FARM
BOWLAND-WITH-
LEAGRAM
SD 648458

1715 and was outlawed with a price on his head. He went into hiding with other rebels at a place called Holdron Castle in Langden Valley. The last years of his life were spent in seclusion in a farm cottage at Sykes in the Trough owned by the devout Roman Catholic family of Parkingson, one of whose number had taken over the old vaccary at Fair Oak.

Recent aerial photography has identified a large circular earthwork at Fair Oak. It has a surrounding ditch and bank enclosing a raised circular mound of approximately 100 m in diameter. It is through that this feature may refer to Bronze and Iron Age settlement in the area, and could possibly be a village site.

FAIR OAK TO KNOT BARN

Go through the gate on the left of the Gunnary barn and cross the field to pass over stiles onto road. Pass over stile opposite and walk on to Higher Greystoneley via stile.

Greystoneley is an ancient Forest vaccary of Little Bowland. The name refers to the grey shale stone that occurs here, and is of no use for building as it crumbles with time.

HIGHER GREYSTONELEY

The recently converted barn here contains the original oak roof truses and purlings, their shape being most unusual: the king post rises from the tie-beam to support the ridge, and rafters incline from the near the ends of the tie-beam to be received by the king post near its head – standard. But what is surprising is the use of space convex brace members springing from the king post – a superb feature.

Pass through the farmstead and follow the old lane down to ford Greystoneley Brook (footbridge on right).

This is a lovely wooded dell where wild garlic, bluebells and primrose flourish with many kinds of moss – wonderful.

Walk up to pass through Lower Greystoneley via gates, and walk on the Knot Barn house.

KNOT HILL LIME KILN & QUARRY

Most kilns in Bowland belong to the 18th and 19th centuries and have mostly been disused for more than a century.

Their basic function is to burn limestone to lime, and this is done in one

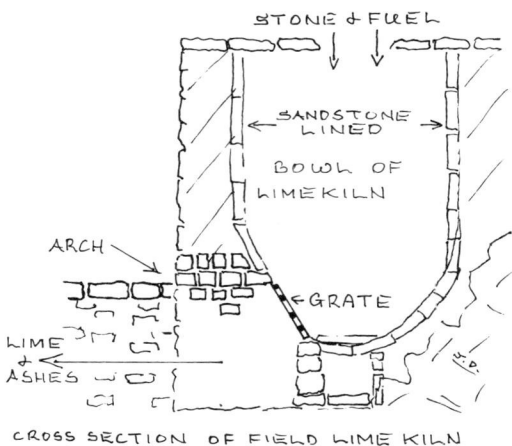

CROSS SECTION OF FIELD LIME KILN

single burning or in a continuing process in which the limestone is fed to the kiln from above and the lime drawn out from the base, regularly and repeatedly over a long period – a 'running kiln'.

The recently restored kiln at Knot Hill is a Running Kiln. The core of the structure is a circular bowl 8-10ft in diameter, lined with sandstone, parallel-sided for the first 6-8ft of its depth, and tapering to a bottom diameter of about 3ft. At the bottom of the bowl a grate was inserted through which the burnt lime and ashes could be racked.

The grate was at the end of a short tunnel, the mouth of which is the arch which gives the kiln its unmistakable character.

Fuel (timber or coal) and limestone was fed in alternately from the top. This kiln is below the quarry from which its limestone supply could be transported with the greatest economy of labour.

The product of the kiln was used in two principal ways – either to make mortar for building or to spread on the land as a manure and to reduce the acidity of a sour soil.

Other uses of lime include; treatment of hides to remove hair, additive for cattle food, making steel and asphalt, flux for smelting and limewash.

INSIDE LIME KILN

KNOT BARN TO CHIPPING

Walk on past the kiln and after passing the quarry cross the field directly to pass over fence-stiles and ditch. Walk down the banking to pass over footbridge.

Notice the line of an old mill race that once fed the water-wheel at Leagram paper mill.

Cross the old mill race and walk up to go over stile. Walk directly on, keeping hedge/fence boundary on your right, to climb over two more fence-stiles and a stream. Walk up, over fence stile and on to pass over stile by gate. Cross the field and walk down the drive to the road. Enter the wood on the right via gate and pass through to meet the road again at Leagram Lodge House. Walk down the road to Chipping.

CHIPPING

Chipping is a charming village still laid out on its 17th century plan. The village originated as a market centre during the Roman period of occupation. Wheat, being one of the primary staples of the Roman Army (the Brigantes preferring rye and oats), was cultivated in the newly cleared Vale of the Loud. This brought an age of prosperity to the district and a trading centre was soon established – horses, salt, lime and grain being the major commodities exchanged. With the demise of Roman influence the fields fell into decay and became mossland. Only the place-name, 'Wheatley', attest to Chipping's former 'Golden Wealth'.

THE SUN INN, CHIPPING

I like to take my repast in the yard of the Sun Inn, but all three inns offer good reasonably priced food and beer.

The Cobble Corner Tea Rooms cater for those of a more patisserie nature – very popular with visitors.

WINDY STREET

A visit to the Parish church of St Bartholomew will prove rewarding. A good guide book is available at a small cost.

We will visit Chipping soon in my new book of family walks, 'Chipping and Bleasdale, Bowland Forest'. Aussteiger Walking Guide.

CHIPPING TO LEAGRAM HALL

From the church steps, walk down Talbot Street to go left at the War Memorial. Walk up the road to enter a wooded area after the Lodge House via gate. Pass through the wood to meet the road at the bottom of Leagram Hall drive. Walk up the drive to the entrance avenue of Leagram Hall. Do not walk up to the house as the grounds are private.

CHIPPING

LEAGRAM HALL

Leagram Hall stands on the site of the old deer park lodge, known as The Lawn. During the 16th century a Roman Catholic chapel was established at the Lawn along with a number of priest hiding places.

Those were dark days for members of the Holy Roman Catholic faith, both Leagram and Wolfen Hall hid priests during that time of persecution. It is reputed that St. Edmund Arrowsmith (executed at Lancaster, August 18th, 1628) occasionally ministered at Leagram Hall.

From 1556 up until the late 17th century, the Lawn was used as a dower house of the Shireburns of Stonyhurst. The house was later passed to Thomas Weld and became home of the Jesuits of Liege. Traces of the old chapel still remain in the west wing.

Leagram was once a great deer park surrounded by a dyke, traces of which can still be made out today. Within the park grew many large oaks, but when disparked in 1556, no deer were left and the few oaks which stood were found to be unfit for building.

LEAGRAM HALL TO PARK GATE BRIDGE

Continue on along the drive...

Great views over to the right; Waddington Fell, Weets Hill, Pendle and Longridge Fell rise to greet us.

...to pass Lawn Farm, and on to go right at junction....

Now Parlick, Wolf Fell, Saddle & Burnslack Fells rise before us.

...to the bridge below Park Gate.

Here, by the bridge and waterfalls, you have a choice: to keep under the fells for a while or take the farm lanes to Lickhurst.

1) FELLSIDE ROUTE

Pass through the bridleway gate on the west side of the bridge and walk down to cross Leagram Brook. Walk up to the left to pass through gate. Walk to the left to find a firm path that takes us up and over to meet a track that takes us to Lickhurst farmyard via gate.

2) FIELD LANES

Cross the bridge and walk up past front of the house then go through the gate. Left, and follow track on, through next gate, and on by the fence to pass through gate on right. Follow track down to the ruin of Park Style.

PARK STYLE c.1580

Park Gate and Park Style mark the northern boundary of the old deer park. Park Gate is alive and well in its lovely setting, Park Style is falling in on itself and its bones being laid bare.

The ruined nature of the 18th century building has revealed an earlier building incorporated into the fabric. A cruck-frame roof tree stands open to the stars, sat atop a wall of a building c.1580 containing three sets of mullioned windows. Inside is a stone spiral staircase and other features of note. But on no account go near to inspect the building as it is a VERY DANGEROUS state.

Continue along the farm lane to Lickhurst via field gates.

LICKHURST TO DINKLING GREEN

Walk down the road to pass over footbridge. Walk up the bank to pass over fence-stile. Walk on and over wall-stile by gate. Cross the fields on a slight left diagonal to enter old lane via gate. Walk on to enter Dinkling Green.

ESHENOKE HOUSE

DINKLING GREEN

Words alone are not enough to describe the enchanting setting of this old Bolland hamlet. Totally enclosed by grassy limestone knolls this is truly the Elysium of Lancashire. Upon entering the verdant hollow from Lickhurst you will know exactly what I mean and like me you will want to return here time and time again.

For many years the hamlet was all but deserted and showing signs of ruin, but under the good stewardship of the Duchy of Lancaster, new life is coming to the fore.

The place-name 'Dinkling' is from the Old Welsh 'din-coed', meaning 'fortified place in the wood'. What we are looking at is a very early Celtic settlement site. Evidence of Iron Age activity is known in the area.

The buildings to be seen here reflect an agricultural age that we shall never see again, a 'Time Capsule' of life before the ethic that spawned the Industrial Revolution. The survival of a landscape like this is very important – it gives us an idea of where we came from before becoming slaves to wages.

The houses and farm buildings display many datestones relating to the Harrison family, long time farmers in Bowland.

On entering the hamlet notice the stone head above a doorway on the left. The barn opposite has a room at the rear lit by a small round-headed window that once served as a chapel. To the right, at the bottom of the yard is a doorhead dated 1818 with two love birds above the initials JH*IH – charming. The building on the right was once the schoolhouse and an inspection of the inside revealed a pair of large oak crucks.

Eshenoke House, once the home of the Bleasdale family, has now been restored after decades of standing empty and forlorn. It displays two Tudor doorheads and low mullioned windows along with some lovely colouration in the stonework.

As the hamlet is now occupied, do not go wandering around willy-nilly, but respect folk's privacy. Courtesy and respect are often rewarded.

DINKING GREEN TO WHITEWELL

Pass through the small gate between the garden wall of the higher house and the modern barns to cross the field to go over the fence-stile to the left of the gateway. Walk on, to climb over fence-stile and walk to the left, passing hen huts, to cross a foot-bridge. Walk up and enter the farmyard via gate, and pass through to follow the farm lane, right at junction to Tunstall Ing house. The view from here must bring great joy to those who abide here.

Passing over the cattle-grid, walk into field on left to pass the fence outer corner, and on in the direction of the old quarry opposite then over fence-stile onto road. Left, and pass

through gate on right to walk around the hill and then through lower field gate. Walk down by the right-hand fence to pass through gateway, and follow track down to farm lane via gate.

ALTERNATIVE IF RIVER IS HIGH

Follow the farm lane to the road, then walk down to cross Burholme Bridge. Walk along the road to pass over a stile on the right. This concessionary path follows the boundary hedge to the Inn At Whitewell via kissing-gate & footbridge.

RIVER CROSSING

After looking at the cheese press, walk on to pass through farmyard at New Laund.

New Laund was a keeper's house in the days of Forest deer park.

From the farmhouse go through gate. Walk down to the Hodder and cross the hipping-stones. Pass over stile by gate and walk to the left to go through the water garden via gate. Walk up to the Inn at Whitewell.

> Our Lady of the Fells
> Look down upon your dowry
> Those in hope and trust
> Honest and true to thee shall be

TALBOT STREET, CHIPPING

WALK 4

WHITEWELL TO STAKES

Walk up the road passing the Village Hall to go up steps on the right & through gate. Walk up to the right of the house to the Water Authority tunnel. To the right a good path leads up to pass through the higher gateway. Walk to the right, through iron kissing-gate and walk directly on to pass over fence-stile, and on by line of fence...

Notice the old Deer Park boundary ditch running along below us.

...to pass through field-gate. Walk on to pass through iron kissing-gate. Cross the field to pass through field-gate and on through old iron gate onto road. Left, and walk on to go over stile by gate on right. Cross the field on a left diagonal to meet with a lone wind-lashed hawthorn. Walk on to pass corner of wood, down to cross over stile by gate. Follow the green track on and down the ford a stream by the river.

In the 17th century the Hodder was teeming with trout, grayling and salmon being an important Bolland industry. The fish was sold at a market held at Beatrix above Dunsop Bridge.

Walk on to pass through kissing-gate by gate. Continue on and up then over stile by gate. Walk on to cross stream then walk up to the farm lane via stile.

I like to stop here with Longridge Fell on my back and Pendle peeping through back on my right and take in the long fell view: Left to Right – Parlick Pike, Wolf Fell, Saddle Fell, Burnslack, Fair Oak Fell and Totridge, then dropping to Whitmore Knots and New Laund Hill. Beatrix Fell then rises with Cat Knot and the wooded Browsholme Heights finishing the span.

Walk down the lane to the front of Stakes Farm.

STAKES

Stakes, still thankfully a working farm, takes its unusual name from the palisade of oak pailings which enclosed the old Leagram deer park on the opposite bank of the Hodder.

Built in the Jacobean period the house is T-shaped in plan. In former times another wing existed and the plan would have been H-shaped with opposite doorways set in the horizontal bar.

Over the north door lintel, that is the strangely undated-given that provision for such was made by the mason; is a large inscribed stone tablet with the following Latin Text:

NUNC MEA MOX HUJUS SED POSTEA NEMO SIBI NATUS.

A rough translation would be: NOW THIS IS MINE: SOON THIS IS

OTHERS: AFTERWARDS WHOSE I KNOW NOT: NOBOBY IS BORN FOR HIMSELF.

I am informed by Mrs Clegg of Stakes that an identical tablet is to be found above a farmhouse doorhead in Swaledale.

Stakes was for many years the home of the Astley family, who in the 16th century purchased the manor of Witton in Blackburn and built Stakes Hall there. The Richmond family followed, and it was they who probably built the present home.

The Toulson family came to Stakes when Clement Toulson married Mary Richmond in c.1660. The fact that a woman became the sole heir could explain the uncertainty expressed in the Latin inscription.

DOORHEADS AT STAKES

STAKES TO KNOT BARN

1) ALTERNATIVE IF RIVER IS HIGH.

Walk back to the shed-barn and on through two steel gates. Walk up past the shed-barn, then follow the hedge/fenceline to pass through gateway and on by the line of thorns to enter a field above the Hodder. Walk on and to the left a bit to go over stile at Doeford Bridge.

In spring you will see the white star-like wood anemone, known as the 'wind flower', by the hedgerow here. It is of great beauty and delicacy and would be much sought after if it were rare. By the stile you will find 'lambs tails' – hazel catkins.

Cross the bridge and follow the road to cross Loud Mytham Bridge.

LOUD MYTHAM HALL

Loud Mytham is a large yeoman farmhouse of the early 17th century that incorporates an earlier timber-framed building – an oak mullioned window was found when work was done on the east wall. Stone mullioned windows abound, and originally the house had many more, as one can make out by inspecting the gable. The Weld family who live here hope to open-up these former lights and we may soon see the house as it was when the old Catholic family of Crombleholme lived here.

In 1534, Edward Crombleholme was paid 26s. 8d. for making 160 roods of paling to be placed above Leagram Deer Park foss (ditch). Edward is also recorded as felling oaks in a place above Wardsley called Aklaye, the 'ack' being a reminder of the many oaks that used to be in the Forest then.

The Crombleholmes were followed by the Marsdens from around 1620 to 1720. Then in turn were followed by the Slater family.

An account is preserved by the Slater family of 'two rebel officers calling at their house' of Loudmytholme, after the retreat from Derby in the Jacobite Rising of 1745, asking for shelter and 'to be directed to the King's Road' to Lancaster.

Many people in the Ribchester-Chipping area supported the Jacobite cause, and in Chaigley there are the remains of a barracks in which Hanoverian soldiers were stationed in order to quell any insurgency within the district.

The 'Stoneyhurst Magazine' of July, 1885, gives the following account; "The country was laid under Martial Law. The luckless insurgents were hunted like wolves amid the neighbouring hills of Preston, and small troops of Hanoverian soldiers were posted throughout the country in bands, and vigorously enforced their presence on the unfortunate exiles. At Chaigley, one of these barracks was established. It is now in ruins, roofless, dilapidated, ivy grown, and is still pointed out as the seat whence the soldiery sallied forth to harass the lands and humble abodes of the outlaws."

Walk up the road and pass through third field gate at corner. Cross the field to corner of fence and walk on to go over stiles by the pond. Cross the track and continue on to corner of wood. Walk by the wood to go over a stile hidden by a holly tree, to the right of Townley House. Then over next stile onto lane. Follow the lane to the road.

You can go up the track on the right of the house opposite to Knot Barn. But I prefer to go past the Old Smithy and by Leagram Mill Farm.

Left, and walk on to pass over stile on right at farm. Walk on to go over stream and footbridge, then walk up to the left to go over wall-stile by 'double-tree'.

THE TOLKIEN TREE

Here we have a mature ash and alder, seemingly growing from the same root. Competing once for the same space, they are now happily espoused.

If only this twin tree was a 'Tree of Tales', and in Autumn carpet the floor with its countless foliage. What a joy it would be to collect a few fallen leaves, some torn and decayed, others fresh off the bough, each a unique embodiment of a pattern to form in the mind and imagination a fantasy tale from a 'Forest of Days' past.

Walk up the lane to Knot Barn House.

2) STAKES TO KNOT BARN VIA WARDSLEY

Cross the hipping-stones and walk on to Wardsley via bridge and gate.

I very much like the old farmhouse at Wardsley with its walled garden and riverside setting, very traditional and very Lancashire. The barn conversion is the best barn conversion that I know, very well proportioned, and the garden will mature well over time.

Walk up the road to go right at junction and after the 'Double Bend' sign, turn right by the side of the converted barn and follow the track up to Knot Barn House.

KNOT BARN TO FAIR OAK

Follow lane on to pass through Lower Greystoneley farmyard via gates. Walk down to cross the ford or footbridge.

What an enchanting little wood this is. Take note of the many mosses growing on the old walls and the flora on the woodland floor.

Continue on to pass through Higher Greystoneley, along the farm lane to the road.

Over to the right is 'The Telephone Box in the Middle of Nowhere', as many know it.

Right, and pass over stiles on left. Cross the field to enter Fair Oak by the side of the stone barn.

FAIR OAK FARM

See Walk 3.

FAIR OAK TO WHITEWELL

Go through the farmyard to take the track down and up and along by the trees to pass through the last gate. Follow the fence round to go over ladder stile. A green path leads us up to the right, and over the rim of New Laund Hill...

What a superb view over this section of the Hodder valley; below we see Burholme Bridge linking Lancashire with the old West Riding. In the distance is the mound of Middle Knoll, sentinel to the 'Centre of the Kingdom', flanked by Staple Oak and Beatrix Fells. Over to the right is Kitcham Hill atop Birkett Fell and a fine view over the old Radholme Deer Park.

If you climb to this spot on a good evening in late May, you will be one of many, here to observe what locals call the 'Middle Knoll Phenomenon'.

This occurs during late May and early June when the sun makes its setting over Morecambe Bay. A minute after total sunset in the Hodder Valley a shaft of the sun's final rays strikes through one of the many ravines which bisect the Bowland fells. The light appears to run up Middle Knoll like a forest fire until the whole west side is illuminated. A few moments later the conflagration retreats and dusk takes over the twilight. Could this be the

NEW LAUND

origin of the name of the valley in which the Knoll rises – Brennand, derived from the Old Norse 'the burning one'?

...to go over stile by gate. Continue on and down to New Laund Farm via gate. Right, and pass by the farmhouse to go through gate. Walk down to cross the Hodder by Hipping-stones.

If the river is high follow the alternative given in Walk 3.

Pass over stile by gate and walk to the left to go through water garden via gates. Walk on to the Inn at Whitewell.

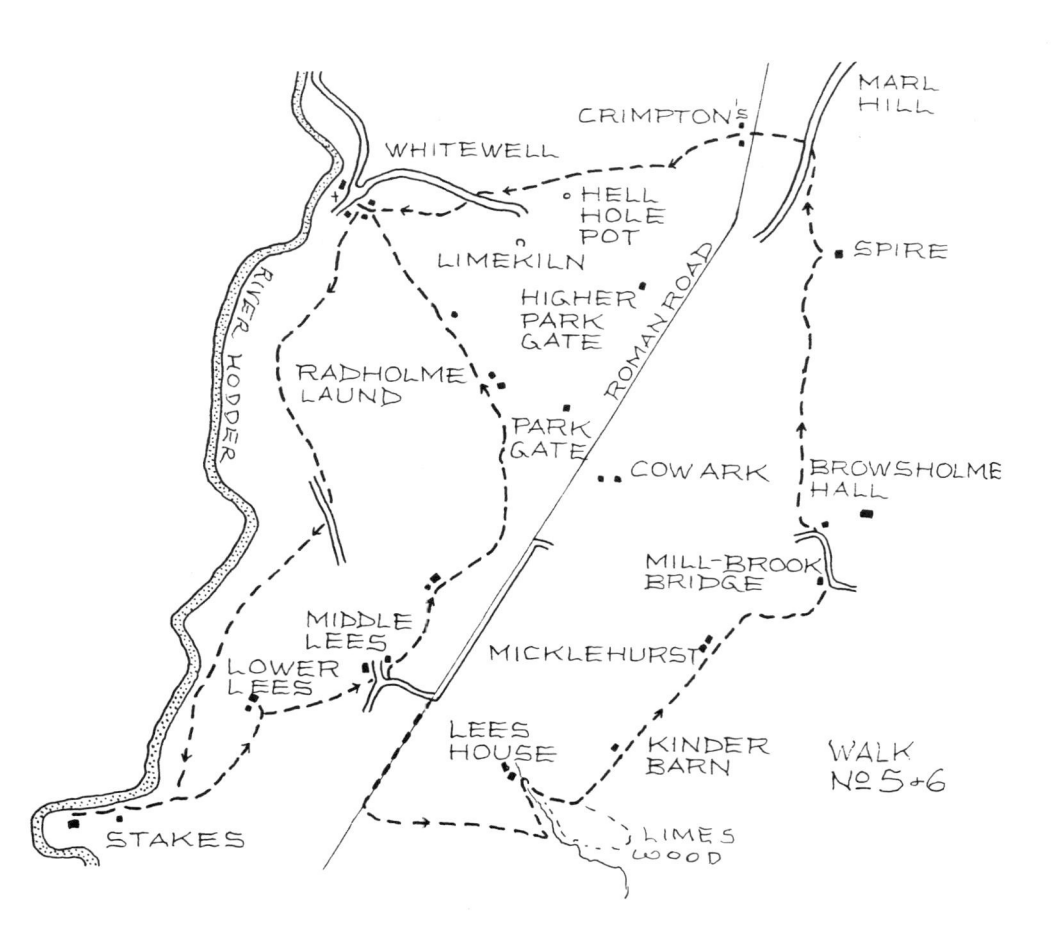

Little Bowland, Lower Hodder Valley & Trough of Bowland 49

WALK 5 & 6
ONCE DEER DID ROAM & ROMANS MARCH

Walk 5, 5 miles, takes in Stakes, the Lees and Radholme Laund.

Walk 6, 9 miles, takes in Stakes, the Lees and Browsholme.

Both walks introduce us to that delightful rustic area between the Bowland Fells and Longridge Fell recorded in the Domesday Book as 'Sotelie' – the Lees. Good dale walking amid superb countryside.

Car parking down to the left of the church.

WALK 5

WHITEWELL TO STAKES
Follow directions in Walk 4.

STAKES TO LOWER LEES
Return up the lane and back over the stile by gate. Walk directly on to ford a stream. Walk on and to the left to pass over fence-stile. Follow left-hand boundary to the farm lane above Lower Lees.

LOWER LEES

The Lees, recorded in the Norman Survey of 1086 as 'Sotelie' – 'the woodland clearing of Sote (Old Norse personal name)' – comprises five farmsteads; Higher Lees, Middle Lees, Lower Lees, Lees House and Stakes.

The lovely whitewashed farmstead of Lower Lees is how I remember farms looking in my childhood, a true farm and a delight to behold.

The decorated doorhead bears the date 1678 with the initials A. R. E., being those of the Rathmell family. The continuous string moulding adds to the charm. In the garden are several old troughs an ancient grindstone. May it long remain a working farm.

LOWER LEES TO MIDDLE LEES

Walk up the lane, left at junction to go around the farmhouse and on by fence to pass through kissing-gates at wood.

Lower Lees

Lots of slate-coloured guineafowl here along with bantam chickens.

Walk on and down to the left to find gate by weir at fancy garden. This foolish gated way leads us to the road at Middle Lees.

MIDDLE LEES

It is a sign of the times as the farming and rural community continue to decline that we see suburban encroachment into an agrarian landscape. But on the brighter side primroses, wild garlic, wood anemones and butterbur still surround this tamed enclave.

Middle Lees

The substantial house here was built by the Towneley family during two periods recorded on shields set into the front gables.

Notice the old milestones set into the walls by the bridge.

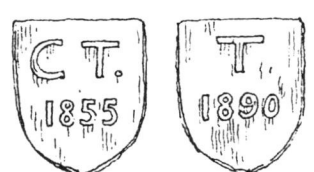

MIDDLE LEES TO RADHOLME LAUND

Walk up the Clitheroe road to pass over stile on left after beech hedge. Walk down to cross the stream and follow it up to go over fence-stile. Walk on upstream to go over fence-stile by holly bush and continue upstream, with a bit of toing and froing, then walk up to enter farmyard via field-gate. From the front of Higher Lees Farm go directly on up an old lane to where it bends to the left. Cross the field directly to go over stile by gate and walk up to the left to pass over wall-stile by wood. Follow wall around the wood and on up through gateway at Radholme Laund. Walk on to view house.

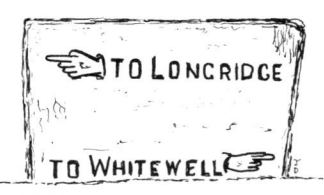

RADHOLME LAUND

During the 13th century the conversion of a large part of the Forest of Bowland to vaccaries and pasture hastened its decline as an open hunting ground. This led to the creation of deer parks at Leagram, and Radholme. Radholme Park lay on limestone rising to over 600ft. on the east bank of the Hodder, north, south and east of Whitewell.

The boundary, consisting of a ditch and a bank, can be reconstructed from place-names and records of old tenures. It ran east from near the confluence of Withens Brook and the Hodder at Ing Wood to Park Gate Farm, then north past Higher Park Gate Farm and over the high ground of Burholme Moor, turning west to join the Hodder below Burholme Farm. It then ran south above the river.

The park boundary consisted of a ditch of 8ft. wide and 4½ft. deep, with the earth thrown up on the outer side to form a bank which was surmounted by a fence of stakes or 'pales' of split oak, on either side of which were three rows of thorns. Gaps in the fences allowed deer to be released into the forest for hunting as required. The pales were in constant need of renewal and the demand for timber quickly depleted the resources of the park.

Custody of the park was undertaken from a lodge, which was the only habitation in the grounds until the 16th century. The building would have been an oak cruck timber construction with a thatched roof. The lodge at Radholme stood on the present site of the Georgian edifice of Radholme Laund.

The park was exclusively for hunting/breeding for only a short period of history being gradually transformed later into rented pastures. The cattle enclosures were surrounded by hedged banks lower than those surrounding the park, but high enough to contain the cattle while allowing free passage to the deer.

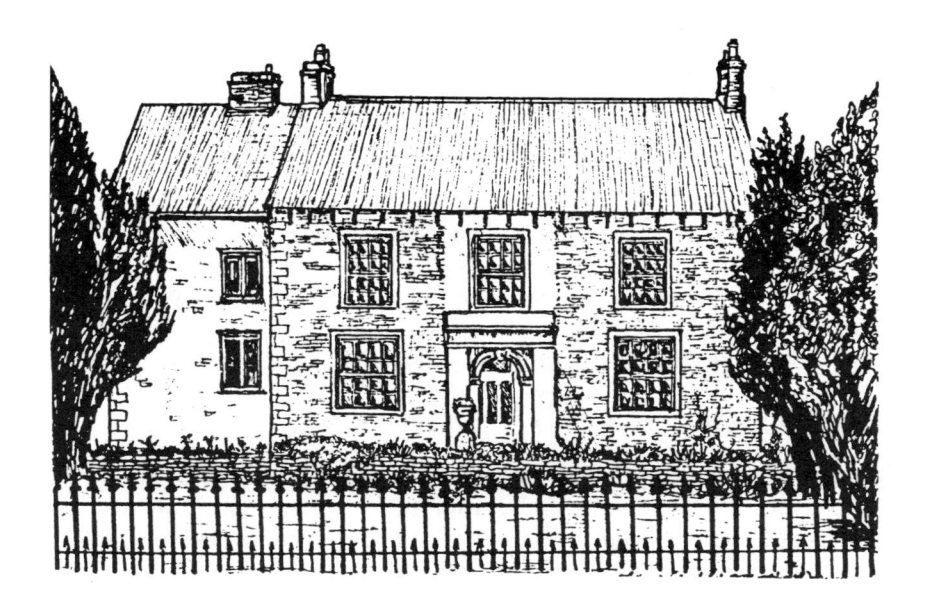

The leasing of the vaccaries and deer parks began the process of the destruction of the game and woodlands of the Forest. Although tenants were not allowed to erect fences against the deer and were prohibited from hunting and killing them, the number of deer declined because little attempt was made to enforce the regulations.

Only in the time of the de Lacy lordship was Bowland regarded primarily as a hunting ground. After it had passed to the Earldom and Duchy of Lancaster the new lords showed little interest in the area and rarely hunted here. The deer became the prey of the tenants and local gentry and unrestricted poaching whittled away their numbers.

The woodland was similarly destroyed, for the demands made upon it exceeded its power of regeneration. The rate of removal was such that by the early 16th century timber was beginning to be in very short supply. It is from this time onwards that we see stone being used as the major building material within the region.

Destruction in the countryside today comes from the strangulation of the majority of broadleaved trees in Lancashire by the unrestricted spread of ivy – Hedera helix, and mechanical hedge cutting by Lancashire County Council –strange that they destroy so many hedgerows and habitat, then at a later date award large grants for their re-laying.

Well, there's the Lancashire Jacobite rising within me.

Looking south over the Lancashire hills the impressive house at Radholme commands a fine prospect fronted by seven yews. To find out who acquired and built this fine house look at he arms displayed in the doorway arch.

RADHOLME LAUND TO WHITEWELL

Enter farmyard by steel field-gate and walk up past the barns into field. Follow right-hand wall up, through old iron kissing gate and then through next iron kissing-gate-cum-stile. Follow left-hand wall on the down...

Good views over the valley between Whitewell and Dunsop.

...to pass over wall-stile. Walk down to Seed Hill drive. Cross drive and walk down to pass through small gate by the new burial ground. Walk down the steps and on down to Whitewell.

In the wooded area below the Village Hall a stream rises to leave the wood by a wall culvert and form a pool from which pheasant drink. The water leaves the pool through the exposed root of a tree and flows under the road to pour out into the White Well at the house below the banking.

On a quite day, lift your eyes and ears, you may spot the pied flycatcher or hear the hoot of the long-eared owl.

WALK 6

WHITEWELL TO MIDDLE LEES, via STAKES & LOWER LEES

Follow directions in Walk 4 to Stakes, then Walk 5 to Middle Lees.

MIDDLE LEES TO LEES HOUSE

Walk up the Clitheroe road to meet with the line of the Roman Road at junction. Right, and walk down the Roman Road track for some way...

The area covered by the Lees is bisected by the Roman military way which runs from Ribchester to Overborough, and for the greater part of its length the road is still in use today passing over Cow Ark.

...to go over plank-bridge and stile on left. Cross the field directly to enter hollow and cross stream. Walk up to the left to go over fence-stile. Walk directly on to edge of plantation to pass over fence-stile. Walk on and cross the field to go over footbridge.

Good views of Pendle and the length of Longridge Fell.

Cross the field directly to pass over fence-stile, then walk to the left to meet with a green lane. Left, and follow the lane to Lees House drive via gates.

LEES HOUSE

Once again we observe suburban encroachment, but in this case it is keeping with the rural landscape and is an example to others – well done.

The Jacobean farmhouse of Lees House has been well restored. The frontage displays a fine array of mullioned windows and the doorhead is of three-arch design with a date tablet above; R. B. 1678.

The vaccary of Lees House was the earliest settlement in the area when Robert Bleasdale enclosed land here in 1609.

Beyond the ravine at Lees House is Limes Wood – anemones, wood sorrel, primroses and violets, bluebells and red campions flourish along with other varieties of flora.

LEES HOUSE TO BROWSHOLME HALL

Our path goes by the side of the house above the wooded ravine to pass over a footbridge then descend steeply, through the holly and wild garlic, to pass over a footbridge and stile by gate into Limes Wood.

Limes Wood is a Public Nature Reserve for rare varieties of wild flowers – see sign for area covered.

The path leads round and up through right-hand gate. Cross the stream and pass over fence-stile. Walk on following left-hand boundary to go through gate at Kinder Barn. Follow the farm lane to where it veers to the left and pass through left-hand field-gate. Walk directly on the enter Micklehurst farmyard via gate. Follow farm lane to where it bends up to the right and go through field-gate on left. Walk down to the right to the road at Mill Brook Bridge via gate. Cross the bridge and walk on...

The cottage on the right has a datestone, 1701, In the gable.

...to the gatehouse of Browsholme Hall.

BROWSHOLME HALL

Browsholme was originally a vaccary (cattle farm) within the Royal Forest of Bowland. It was sold by Elizabeth 1 to the duke of Devonshire and was eventually acquired by the tenant, Thomas Parker whose family had been park keepers at Radholme Laund – well positioned when Crown leases and property were being sold to raise money for the State.

The family prospered in their business and property dealings and acquired the trappings of the diminished master forester's office and subsequently held it as hereditary.

The history of the Parkers of Browsholme provides a portrait of the rise of the yeoman gentry in the post-Reformation era and their survival to the present day – a tome too weighty to cover in my little work.

The Hall is a superb example of a Jacobean country house. It has a symmetrical red sandstone front with two short projecting wings. The centre is taken by a frontpiece superimposed orders of Classical couple columns; Doric, Ionic and Corinthian.

The Hall is furnished in keeping with the period and holds some unusual antiquities, and along with splendid grounds is well worth a visit between May and August when there are Open Days. Tel: 01254 826714 for details.

BROWSHOLME HALL TO THE SPIRE

Enter drive on left of gatehouse to go through gate on left. Follow track up to pass over stile by gate beyond the cattle-grid. Walk up the field to go over stile by gate at corner of wood. Walk up the track and then through field-gate. Walk up to the right to go over stile by gate at pond. Walk towards the left of the Spire to pass over fence-stile by pinewood.

THE SPIRE

The Spire at Browsholme Heights is a folly built by the Parkers of Browsholme to act as a landmark for shooters on the fells. It consists of a castellated wall with a central Gothic arch, the latter is now bricked up. From a distance it gives the appearance of a church tower.

THE SPIRE

THE SPIRE TO CRIMPTON

Follow the path to the farm lane...

Good view of the Hodder Valley with Ingleborough, Pen-y-Ghent and Great Whernside in the distance.

...and walk into the field and down to the right to pass over fence-stile at wood. Walk down through the pines and onto road via stile. Walk along Crimpton Drive to front of

farmhouse.

The concessionary, muddy diversion is only optional.

CRIMPTON

Known as 'Our Lady of the Fells' the farmstead of Crimpton is now holiday cottages. What a lovely spot this is for those wishing to spend some time exploring the Hodder Valley.

CRIMPTON TO WHITEWELL

Pass through the farmyard to leave by field gate.

A lovely view of the wooded Kitcham Hill and the fells beyond.

Walk on to pass through gates and across the field to enter plantation at inner corner via stile. Pass through the pines to leave by stile and ladder-stile.

Once again, superb views over the fells from Parlick to Totridge above 'The Old Man of Bolland'.

Walk down to the right of the trees that surround Hell Hole pot. Continue on down to pass over stile and ladder-stile near gateway. Walk to the left to go over stile by gate onto road. On through gate opposite and walk across to the right to pass through field gate. Walk down by the line of trees to pass the rear of Seed Hill Farm onto farm track. Walk down the grassy bank and on through small gate on the left of the new burial ground. Walk down steps and on down to Whitewell.

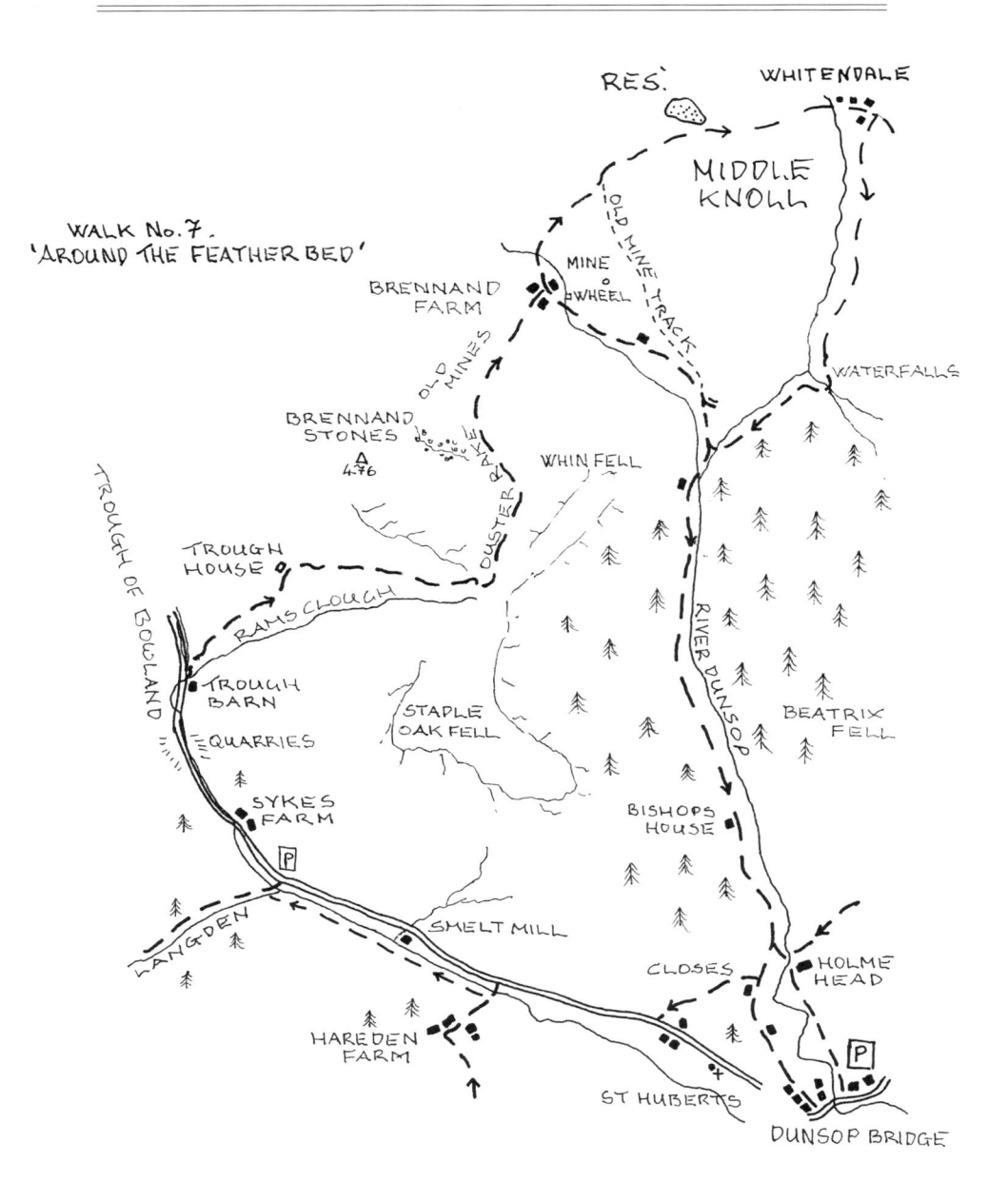

WALK No. 7.
'AROUND THE FEATHER BED'

WALK 7
AROUND THE FEATHER BED

7 or 9 miles good walking with hill climbs and superb views. Allow 5 or 6 hours to include a picnic lunch.

This walk takes us into Trough of Bowland to climb steadily over Whins Brown to the remote settlements of Brennand and Whotendale – the 'Heart of Bowland' at the 'Centre of the Kingdom'. We return by a riverside path reminiscent of a Scottish glen in all its glory.

Follow directions in Walk 1 to Hareden Bridge.

Walk up the tree-lined avenue to pass over a fence-stile on the right. Cross the bridge up to your left and walk back down the field to pass over a stile on the riverbank.

On the walk by the river lookout for the grey wagtail, dipper, sand martin and sand piper throughout the spring and summer.

DUNSOP BRIDGE

A path leads us upriver to pass over a stile. A good path leads us through the tussocky grass...

The building up on the right is Smelt Mill Cottages, home now to the Bowland Pennine Mountain Rescue Team. Nearby are the low remains of a former smelt mill that served both the Sykes and Brennand lead mines, the Brennand ore being transported over Whin Fell by way of the Ouster Rake track.

...to pass over a stile and bridge onto the Langden Intake drive via gate.

There are many good high fell walks to be had from the Langden Valley, and the serious walker is well aware of the options – see WALK 8.

Walk down the drive to follow the road to Skyes.

SYKES

In 1332 the family of Adam Langto are recorded as tenants of the vaccary (Stock Farm) of Glastirdale – now the roadside hamlet of Sykes in Losterdale. By 1407 the Bonde family, relatives of the Langtos, were tenants up to a time when in the late 17th century the Parkinson family took over the tenure.

The Parkinsons built the hamlet much as we see it today. Their initials are recorded on two decorated doorheads and on a date tablet above a cowshed door.

The Parkinsons of Bolland and Bleasdale have always been strong adherents to the Roman Catholic Faith, recorded as recusants and being involved in the Rebellions of 1715 & 1745.

During those troubled times Sykes became a refuge for those outlawed by the Crown. The outlaws had their hideaway high above the Langden Valley at a place later named Holdron Castle.

SYKES FARM 1692

In later times Sykes became a roadside stop for travellers to and from Lancaster along the Trough road, and a wayside inn came into being.

During World War 11 a searchlight unit was based on the flat land below Sykes, manned by twelve men.

SYKES TO BRENNAND
Continue along the Trough road to the roadside lime kiln.

This lime kiln was in use into 20th century, and is of a kind as described at Knot Barn, below Greystoneley.

On either side above the road here are two quarries in the core of Sykes anticline, a fold running for some miles to the north east; notice that the rock strata in this section of the Trough are steeply tilted and in places very much bent. In the eastern quarry the folding and contortions in the strata are very well displayed.

In the 19th century a small mine worked three lead veins in the western quarry and the position of the mines can still be made out as a series of small openings near the top of the quarry face.

Inspect the kiln, but remember, the quarries are OUT OF BOUNDS.

We walk on to cross a lovely stone bridge...

A cartload of Lancashire witches passed this way in 1612 to suffer their fate at Lancaster. In the case of those from Pendle it was a vile plot of the local Protestant gentry to strike a final blow to the Catholic branch of the Nutter family – Alice Nutter, a Gentlewoman in her eighties, was the mother of Robert and John Nutter, both Roman Catholic priests who faced martyrdom.

...then pass over a stile by gate at Trough Barn. The track leads us up to the ruin of Trough House.

Trough House stands above the deep ravine of Ughter Syke, now known as Rams Clough, from which the Ouster Rake and Sykes take their names.

Ughter Skye and Ouster Rake are part of the ancient Harrington Dike, one of the oldest landmarks in Bolland. The Dike marked the southern boundary of land held by the Harringtons of Hornby Castle.

I only distantly remember the farm being occupied: the farmer's wife, who was never lonely as she had the gift of conversing with trees, gave myself and my friend John Mitchell a cool glass of milk each to see us over to Brennand.

During my survey for this walk, March 2004, a red kite watched from a branch as I smoked my roll-up of fine Dutch tobacco.

Continue up the track to pass over stile by gate and walk on by the silver birch plantation out beyond the wall onto the moor. A staked path leads us up to pass through a wall-gate. On up we go to pass over a stile by gate on the ridge of Whin Fell. We now follow the Ouster Rake track to descend...

What an awe-inspiring view laid before us. You can almost reach out and hug Middle Knoll, on whose flanks are to be found signs of settlement and mining activity going back to Roman times.

...to the Brennand pastures via gate. Continue on down to pass through field-gate. On we go down to pass through gate and over ladder-stile by gate into the farmyard at Brennand.

BRENNAND

Brennand Farm stands in one of the remotest and picturesque settings in Bowland, an ancient vaccary established by the monks of Whalley Abbey.

Up to the late 17th century the farmhouses of Bolland were primitive cruck-framed structures open to the roof divided into two or three rooms. The barns, again cruck-framed, are described in 1652 as 'large open church-like structures....made of large baulks of timber, entire oak trees, springing from

Brennand Farm

a low wall and meeting in the centre in a pointed arch'. The roof would have been thatched.

Few remanents of these buildings survive today and are mostly to be found incorporated in 17th century stone rebuilds as at Loud Mythan, Park Style and Wolfen Hall.

Brennand Stone

It is recorded in Whalley Abbey documents of c.1347, 'that there was once in Bouland a certain chapel called Brennand Chapel, which chapel belonged to the parish church of Whalley'.

Supporting this tradition is a stone inscribed with the Christian monogram HIS – Greek letters for Jesus, and five crosses, found some sixty years ago at Brennand Farm. This 12th century alter stone is today built into the alter in the chapel at Whalley Abbey.

Standing near to the farm is an old mahogany-panelled grouse keepers' cabin. During the breeding season a keeper had to spend some time on the fells warding off predators that steal the eggs, and prey on the young. At such times the wheeled cabin would be provisioned and horse-drawn onto the fells, providing the keeper with a mobile living place. During the game season it also served as a refreshment cabin for the shoot.

In past years grouse have been scarce on the fells, falling prey to hawks and other wildlife. Recent years, due to good land management, numbers have increased and more shoots are again being organised on the fells.

Though I do not myself agree with the ethos behind modern day field sports, and the vain show of wealth that goes with it. I do strongly agree with the countryside management that goes with it and the local employment it provides. And until the worm turns that will have to do.

BRENNAND TO WHITENDALE

Pass through the farmyard and follow the walled track to cross the Brennand River. Walk up the track on the right, left at

the junction and on to pass over stile by gate. Continue up to top junction and go left to pass over stile by gate near wall. The path runs by the wall, then crosses a stream, and on to go over a stile.

The workings that we have just passed are the spoil heaps and low remains of buildings known as 'The Kings Silver Mines in Bolland'. These were first worked by Sir Belvis Bulmer in 1610, who 'brought the mine to great perfection, and getting great store of Silver Ore'.

We shall soon pass the reservoir that once gave a head of water to power the crusher. The water-wheel pit stands by the river opposite Brennand Farm.

The mines lie off the path and should NOT BE APPROACHED as they present GREAT DANGER.

This area, known as 'Good Grave', has been mined for lead and silver since Roman times, and a Romano-British settlement site is located on the Whitendale side of Middle Knoll.

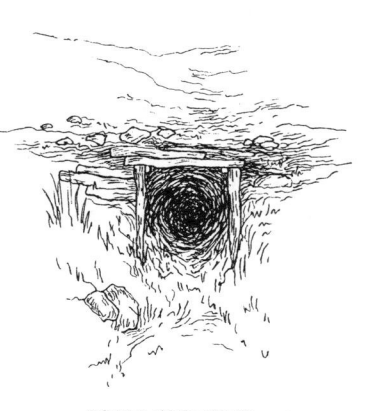

BRENNAND MINE

Walk on over the rough ground, passing the reservoir...

To the north-west, beyond the brow of Good Greave, lies the exact Centre of Great Britain determined by the O.S. to be at NGR SD 63770 56550. The Whitendale Hanging Stones, a dramatic outcrop of wind-lashed gritstone some 600m east, are used as a depiction of this point.

Souvenir walking and information cards can ONLY be obtained from Puddleducks Post Office & Tea Room at Dunsop Bridge. The frontispiece being a print of the celebrated oil painting by the renowned Lancashire artist David N. Johnson – 'The Whitendale Hanging Stones'.

...down to go through wall gate. Walk down the steep track to cross the river bridge at Whitendale.

WHITENDALE

'The Dale of the White Heather' – what a lovely setting; an oasis of green secluded by the wild high fells.

An old monastic road once ran through here to meet the Hornby Road, a salt way of old, once marked by the now lost Whitendale Cross.

The short-eared owl is a common sight in the dale. The Twitcher, with its two large glass eyes, is a regular visitor. Notice its subdued plumage.

WHITENDALE TO DUNSOP BRIDGE

Pass through the upper farmyard and follow the wall around to the right to pick up a good track that takes us to the footbridge over the waterfalls via gates.

Standing upon the bridge above the tumbling waters, we look up to view the enchanted Fairy Glen.

Tales of elves and fairy folk abound in Bowland lore, like those who dance and sing at Dinkling Green, or those who wash their tiny garments by moonlight at Whitewell.

Here at Costy Clough the tiny folk come to drink and bathe in the twilight just before moonrise, their songs in rhythm with the cascading waters.

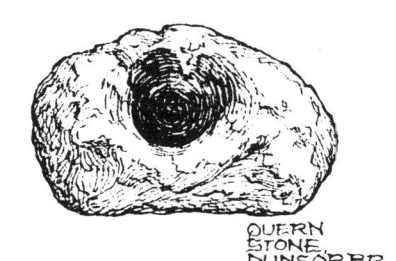

QUERN STONE, DUNSOP BR.

Follow the path on and down the zigzags to walk downriver to cross a footbridge. Return down the access road to Dunsop Bridge.

Walking along the pine-lined valley we could easily be in the wild

Highlands of Scotland – enjoy the wind-down.

By the side of the river are some revered alders:

> 'Alder for shoes do wise men chose,'
> *Rudyard Kipling*

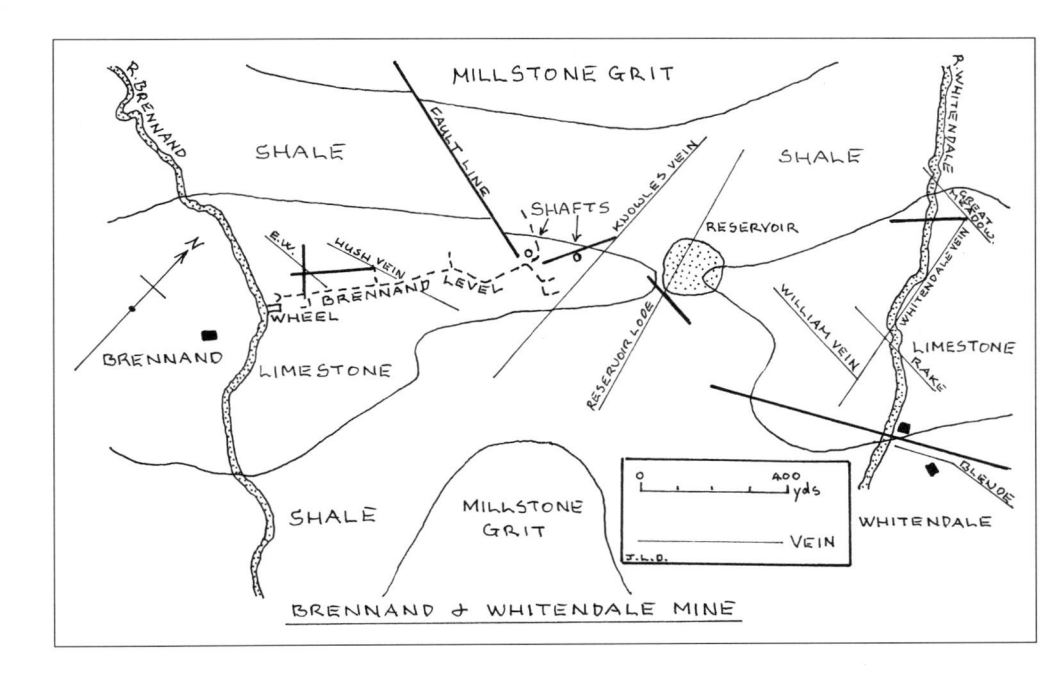

BRENNAND & WHITENDALE MINE

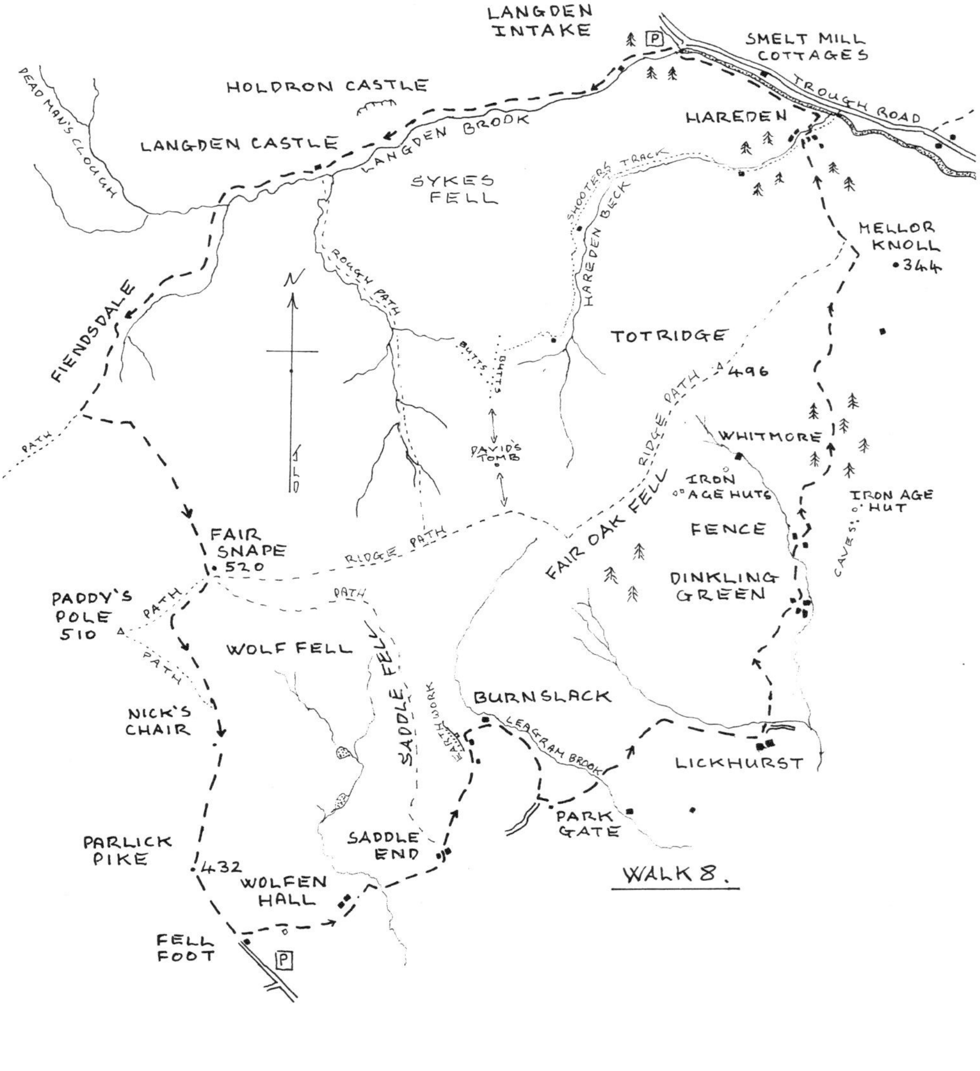
LANGDEN INTAKE
P
SMELT MILL COTTAGES
TROUGH ROAD
HOLDRON CASTLE
DEAD MAN'S CLOUGH
LANGDEN CASTLE
LANGDEN BROOK
HAREDEN
SYKES FELL
SHOOTERS TRACK
HAREDEN BECK
MELLOR KNOLL
•344
ROUGH PATH
N
FIENDSDALE
TOTRIDGE
BUTTS
BUTTS
496
PATH
RIDGE PATH
WHITMORE
DAVID'S TOMB
IRON AGE HUTS
IRON AGE HUT
CAVES
FAIR SNAPE
•520
RIDGE PATH
FENCE
FAIR OAK FELL
PADDY'S POLE
510
PATH
PATH
DINKLING GREEN
WOLF FELL
SADDLE FELL
PATH
BURNSLACK
EARTH WORK
NICK'S CHAIR
LEAGRAM BROOK
LICKHURST
PARK GATE
SADDLE END
PARLICK PIKE
432
WOLFEN HALL
WALK 8.
FELL FOOT
P

WALK 8
HEART OF BOWLAND

"And if we strive to live the lives our fathers lived of yore,
Old England once again may be what England was before."
— *an aspiration from the 'Lancashire Broughton Song'*

Park your car at Langden Intake or walk up from Dunsop Bridge using the directions given in Walks 1 & 7.

Distance in miles is not important here. All that is needed is a stout-heart (and boots), victuals and a full day.

The lengthy valley approach to the summit of Fair Snape Fell is a walk that you never want to end, such is the sense of solitude and well-being provided by the wilderness here. The ling and fern-clothed valley sides soar steeply upwards and one feels drawn into the very heart of the untamed Bowland hills.

The return from Parlick Pike, through a land below the fells high above the Loud and Hodder, is a joy of rustic landscapes – green meadows and rolling hills with here and there a friendly farmstead. Alone or in good company this makes for a rewarding and enjoyable full-day out.

LANGDEN INTAKE TO LANGDEN CASTLE

Follow the conifer-lined lane to the lovely setting of Langden Intake Waterworks. After passing through a gate a good track leads us on into the wild valley, and then to climb a shooters track to above the trees. Here we take the lower track that runs just above the valley floor to its high point by the finger post.

Above us, almost hidden by the trees, is a natural shelf once the redoubt of a band of Jacobite Outlaws who named their place of refuge Holdron Castle. Their fortified shelters were destroyed long ago and the place became a stone quarry.

Here, concealed deep within the Bowland wilderness, the remnants of those who stood with Colonel Francis Towneley at Carlisle, and others from the Borders who had sought refuge in Lancashire after Culloden, carried on their rebel calling.

Such were their actions that the County was laid under Martial Law and troops of Hanoverian soldiers were posted throughout the region. These bands hunted the outlaw insurgents like wolves and vigorously enforced their presence on the Lancashire folk, who cherished a faithful devotion to the bold and unfortunate exiles.

Many of those taken the '45 were granted the King's Mercy of Transportation and perpetual banishment to his Colonies of North America and the islands of the Caribbean where they were used as indentured labour for the rest of their lives – slaves.

In the West Indies the Jacobite blood of these dreadlocked Northern recusants was often mixed with that of their brother African, and two hundred years later their descendants brought back to the United Kingdom the name and blood of many Northern and Scottish families.

It might well be that the great Bob Marley owes more to 'The Lion of the North' than 'The Lion of Judaea'.

> My Bonny lies over the ocean,
> My Bonny lies over the sea.
> My Bonny lies over the ocean,
> Will you bring my Bonny to me....

Walk down to Langden Castle

LANGDEN CASTLE

Langden Castle stands in an oasis of green at the foot of Bleadale Water. Though only a simple shooters hut today, a larger building served as a shooting lodge in the 19th century.

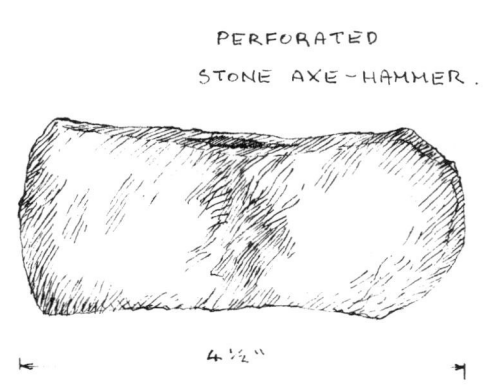

PERFORATED STONE AXE-HAMMER.

4 ½"

A stone axe hammer, with an hourglass perforation, was found in Langden Brook in 1988. This valley route would have been well known to those Iron/Bronze Age communities at Dinkling Green and Bleasdale.

The Harrington Dike that we talked about in walk 7, was part of greater man-made ditch and vallum earthwork, built in the Iron Age to control cattle and act as a boundary, that ran from Settle to Garstang. Beyond Fiendsdale are sections of this once great earthen boundary way, that made good use of natural features, referred to on the OS as Calder Dykes.

LANGDEN CASTLE TO FAIR SNAPE FELL

Continue along the track, then after crossing a stream, walk on to pick up a path on the left that will lead us over to the bottom of Fiendsdale.

What evil spirit or demon lives here?

Here the Langden Brook, having left its 'feather bed' to flow through Dead Man's Stake Clough, meets with Fiendsdale Water. And what a good story these combined waters could tell.

We cross at the confluence and follow the path up the nab to traverse Fiendsdale to its head. We now pass through a peat hag landscape to emerge below the ridge fence line. Walk on to go over fence-stile at Fiendsdale Head. Follow the fence to the left to the summit cairn (over fence).

FAIR SNAPE FELL

Fair Snape Fell has two summits: we are stood on the highest at 520m, Paddy's Pole to the south-west, is 10m lower but makes up for its short stature by having a Trig. Point and stone wind shelter.

FAIR SNAPE FELL TO PARLICK PIKE

Pass over the ladder-stile and walk to the right where a firm path leads over the moor of Wolf Fell to a ladder-stile. Do not pass over. Follow the line of the wall on a good path to climb over ladder-stile by gate. Continue on to the summit cairn.

PARLICK PIKE

On reaching the summit, all your efforts on the long valley ascent are supremely rewarded with extensive and contrasting panoramas. Looking back, the vivid mountain grasses carpet the sleek weather-beaten slopes of Wolf Fell and Fair Snape, which rises from an undulating ridge. Before you the Vale of Chipping and Bleasdale compose a gentle and more verdant landscape, recalling an age of 'Lancashire past' Beyond are the untamed moorland hills of the Palatine that reach down to the coastal plain that flank the Ribble estuary.

> The men that live in North England
> I saw them for a day:
> Their hearts are set upon the waste fells,
> Their skies are fast and grey:
> From their castle-walls a man may see
> The mountains far away.
>
> *Hilaire Belloc*

Parlick, in the past, has been a rallying point for local Catholics, especially during the Jacobite Rebellions of the 18th century. Tales are told of lights burning on the summit at the very dead of night, where men would set their plans against the Hanoverian usurpers. Those of free will, will always hold out against predestination, as one man demonstrated between the Mount of Olives and the Hill of Golgotha.

PARLICK TO WOLFEN HALL

A path leads away from the carin and quickly descends to Fell Foot, where, at the bottom of the steps, a path runs to the left and leads us to the low ruin of Wildcock House via stile. Left, and cross the field, veering to the right to pass over stile by cattle grid above Wolfen Hall. The post-waymarker directs us to the entrance of Wolfen Hall.

WOLFEN HALL

Wolfen Hall was once the old manor house of Chipping, being then the home of John de Knoll of Chippindale, and later passing by marriage to Roger, third son of Robert Shireburn of Stoneyhurst. The Shireburns, along with the Hoghton family, became the largest landowners in the district, both holding rival manorial courts in the village.

In St. Bartholomew Church at Chipping was the Shireburn Chantry Chapel, now the Wolfhouse Quire. This was founded in 1519 by Roger Shireburn and used as a burial place for the family up till the late 17th century.

Recent restoration work at Wolfen Hall has revealed a tall oaken window with long and slender chamfered mullions, part of an older timber-framed house incorporated in the later stone rebuild.

The work also uncovered a previously unknown Priest Hole – hiding-place for Catholic priests in the days of persecution.

WOLFEN HOLE TO DINKLING GREEN

The post way-markers lead us past the front of Wolfen Hall, down over a stile by gate. Cross the field to pass over fence-stile., and on to next fence-stile. Walk down to cross Chipping Brook by footbridge. Follow line of fence up to go over stile by gate.

Turn back for a last look at Parlick.

Walk on by the way-marker posts to pass over higher stile.

On your right is an old War Department marker – W D No.27.

After the Retreat of Dunkirk, June 1940, The British Army re-occupied these former highland strongholds, expecting an imminent invasion by another Hanoverian-backed army.

With the formation of a coalition Cabinet under Winston Churchill the British people rallied in defiant mood, and with the aid of the American Armed Forces went on the crush the Fascist threat.

Sadly, we did not go on to free our former allies, the people of Poland and the Baltic States. Only now, at the time of writing, have they regained their hard-won Freedom and birthright to participate in the making of a free and meritocratic Europe.

Go through the little wood to the drive at Saddle End via stile. Enter and go through the farmyard to follow a track on the right. After passing over a stile by gate, follow the track on to where it enters a field above a barn. Here, take the old hollowed track by the wall, past the barn, on to the ruin of Ward's End.

In the grasses by the ruin of Ward's End are a number of stone window mullions and heads and a sadly broken 17th century decorated doorhead – 1666 P *.

In 1592, Bryan Parker had a dwelling house at Ward's End and is recorded as digging for turf on Saddle Fell. These peaty blocks would have been used to heat the dwelling, and the many rutted tracks that can be seen running along the Saddle are those made by the pony-drawn sledges of the peat diggers.

WARD'S END
WHO CARES ?

On the west side of Burnslack Brook, upon a bank at the east side of the Saddle, is an earthwork known 'Castlestead'. The name is first recorded in a document of 1567. Local farmers then thought it to be a fortress of the Ancient Britons.

Upon inspection, it can be made out as a man-made line running along an extraordinarily steep gradient, an artificial rim high up on the steep side of the Saddle. Behind the shelter of the earthwork you are out of view of those below. But as to what purpose this structure served I can only ponder.

Walk past the ruin and over stile by gate and follow the path to enter Burnslack via gate.

What a great place to live, and much appreciated by the owners.

In the Accounts of Henry de Worsley, Storer of Bolland (1422-23), the farm at Brendslake was granted to John Parker son of Elias Parker for the term of 20 years. Burnslack was then part of the Lickhurst vaccary in Chepynwarde. Thus we have the origin of the name Ward's End.

Follow the garden path, then over a ladder-stile onto drive. Follow the farm drive to the tarmac road. Leave the road to go over a stile by gate, on your left. This moorland track leads us on to cross Leagram Brook by stepping stones, and on over the moor round to Lickhurst Farm via gate.

The old Chipping family of Sartivant are recorded at being at the ancient vaccary of Lickhurst before 1500.

The Act Book of Whalley Abbey from 1510 to 1538 sheds unusual light on family relationships in Little Bolland at the time:

At the court held 30 October, 1518, convened to consider a doubtful marriage between Matthew Parker of Lickhurst and Agnes Sourbutts. Witnesses were called about the forbidden degree of relationship between the two.

"On oath they asserted that James Overend, alias Robinson of Bentham, and Agnes, former wife of John Parker of Lickhurst were brother and sister. The above named James had a son George, who had a daughter Alice, the mother of Agnes Sourbutts. The above named Alice had a son, James Parker, the father of Matthew."

Walk down the road to cross Greystoneley Brook by footbridge. Walk up to pass over fence-stile. Walk on, and over wall-stile by gate. Cross the fields on a slight left-diagonal to enter old lane via gate. Walk on to enter Dinkling Green.

DINKLING GREEN

In her wonderful book 'Three Rivers', Jessica Lofthouse conjures up a romantic fairy tale setting for Dlinkling Green with tales of elves, hobbled folk and fairy rings recounted to her by locals here. I know a few who still recount such tales.

When at Stoneyhurst College Sir Arther Conan Doyle led walks into Little Bolland and knew this setting well.

J.R.R. Tolkien also visited Dinkling Green during his many stays at Stoneyhurst and gained inspiration from these local hill-folk tales for his children's book 'Lord of the Rings'.

If the children's book that I am working on at the moment does half as well, then I shall retire to Dutton in eccentricity.

DINKLING GREEN TO LANGDEN INTAKE

Pass through the small gate between the garden wall of the higher house and the modern barns, to cross the field and over a fence-stile to the left of the gateway. Walk on to climb over fence-stile and keep to the left, passing hen huts, to cross a foot-bridge. Walk up and enter the farmyard at Fence via gate.

The name Fence refers to the ancient deer park fence that was established at New Laund as an extension to Radholme Park. This took place when Edward IV granted the park at Radholme to Robert Harrington of Hornby Castle. The Fence estate included most of the land on the west bank of the Hodder between Dunsop and Whitewell.

Pass through the farmyard to follow the farm lane, left at the junction, to the hen huts as the lane turns up to Whitmore. A path leads to the right to enter Whitmore Plantation via gate. A forest path takes us through the dark deep wood to leave via gate. The path goes down and through the trees to come out by a gate below the Totridge-Mellor Knoll saddle. Walk up to go over a ladder-stile. Our path takes us over the saddle below Mellor Knoll to climb over a stile by gate. Walk directly on down to pass over a stile by gate near Riggs Plantation. Walk down to Hareden via wall-stile and river bridge.

The road leading into the valley leads up to the shooting lodge and butts on Hareden fell, and is a very spectacular walk indeed.

By following the line of butts over some very rough ground you reach the raised mound of David's Tomb and the ridge fence-line. A return over Totridge Fell to the saddle and Hareden makes this walk complete.

When the 'Right to Roam' comes in this year, 2004, this walk may be possible without obtaining permission first.

Pass through the farmyard, over the stone bridge, and on to go over a fence-stile on the left. Cross the bridge up to the left and walk down the field to go over stile onto the riverbank. A path takes us upriver to climb over a stile. A good path takes onto the Intake drive via gate.

> I am fond of Occam's Razor,
> Or the Law of Parsimony, which suggests
> That the simplest explanation of a phenomenon
> Is usually the most trustworthy.
> *Kurt Vonnegut, 1997*